Dedication

To my daughter Miriam Josie, for coming into the world and for being the greatest of gifts, may you be a blessing for others and may you live your life from the inside out.

May the real you shine like a beacon of Light in a dark world, and may you make a difference in this world to usher the age of peace, prosperity, health, and total fulfillment.

You are the Light within my soul and I love you with all my heart.

"You are magnificent when you accept all of who you are without judgment"

Dear reader,

I welcome you into a journey, this is a journey into a realm you know exists, but you may not have developed the knowledge and practical ways to step into it permanently.

By the time you finish reading this book you will have a stronger grasp on some of the greatest secrets to living a life full of bliss, a life that is already within your reach, all you have to do is let the real you live it, and step into a chaos free life.

I can confidently say that after reading the pages of this book, your life will be changed for the better, forever. You may need to read it several times, because your ability to absorb and adopt many of the principles presented will grow as you get closer and closer to activating the real you.

I have personally tested every principle you'll read about, and I have also stumbled onto a short cut to step into a parallel universe where love is pervasive; an undifferentiated reality where the realm of right and wrong, or even cause and effect simply does not exist.

Don't believe anything you read, try it and if it works for you keep doing it; the goal is not to convince you to change your beliefs, the goal is to release you from beliefs that may hold you back from living a chaos free life.

"You are magnificent when you accept all of who you are without judgment"

I only request as you read this book, to not jump ahead. Each chapter builds on the previous, and the next. Sometimes the concepts presented are very arguable, and presented in the form of a theory; I use many metaphors to get you to think. At times the concepts may be hard to grasp, but they will come together in later chapters.

Its best you keep reading even if you have not fully understood a chapter because the ideas become clearer as the puzzle pieces unfold before your eyes and your subconscious mind. I have assimilated this knowledge over many years, both through study and through difficult situations where I have learned in the trenches how to live a chaos free life.

For example, I overcame physical death in 1995, relationship death in 2002, and financial death in 2009. The purpose of this book is to provide you with simple, practical, tried and true ways to activate the real you.

The real you lives in a chaos free reality, by the time you finish reading this book, you'll know how to experience life through the real you.

Love and Light,

Tullio Siragusa

"You are magnificent when you accept all of who you are without judgment"

About the author

Tullio Siragusa began to study history and religious works at the early age of 7; by the time he turned 19 he was already lecturing in public halls about several life topics, and continued on this path till the age of 30.

At the age of 30, Tullio began a deeper dive into the works of philosophers such as Socrates, Plato, Aristotle, and esoteric works of 16th Century Kabbalist such as R. Moshe Chaim Luzzatto, and modern works of R. Philip Berg. Tullio also began to study ancient works such as the Book of Enoch, and King Solomon's writings.

Now into his 40s, Tullio is ready to share the knowledge he's collected but in a practical way for everyday life, some have called Tullio's writings "Practical Wisdom for our Modern Time".

Tullio also managed to lead a successful career as a senior executive for some of the most prestigious firms in the world, and has pushed the limit as an entrepreneur having endured several failures in both business and in his personal life. Tullio brings a very secular view to this book, not just theory; making Tullio a practical scholar.

Born in Switzerland, raised in Italy and having lived in New York, Boston, Philadelphia, Toronto Canada, Monterrey Mexico, London UK, and now residing in Los Angeles, Tullio also brings a very international perspective to his work.

His style of writing helps the reader visualize concepts in pictures, and brings all the puzzle pieces together one by one, until the very end of the book when the big picture comes together for the reader.

The content of this book it is truly applied practical wisdom for our modern time, from someone who's lived in the real world.

"You are magnificent when you accept all of who you are without judgment"

The Real You

Living a Chaos Free Life

By: Tullio Siragusa

"You are magnificent when you accept all of who you are without judgment"

Table of content

"You are magnificent when you accept all of who you are without judgment"

"You are magnificent when you accept all of who you are without judgment"

"You are magnificent when you accept all of who you are without judgment"

Becoming a visionary

Before the Newtonian revolution, people explained the world around them primarily in terms of a God that made specific decisions.

A child would fall and break his arm, and it was an act of God. Crops failed; it was an act of God. People thought God was someone who made each and every specific event happen.

Then in the 1600s people said, "No that's not it, what God did was to put in place the Universe with certain principles, and what we need to do is figure out how those principles work. God doesn't make all the decisions, God set in place processes and principles that would carry on".

From that point on, people began to look for basic underlying dynamics, and principles of the entire Universe. That is what the Newtonian revolution was all about.

Similarly, the Darwinian revolution gave us a dramatic shift in thinking about biological species and natural history, shift in thinking that provides fruitful analogies to what we need develop within, to become visionaries.

Prior to the Darwinian revolution, people primarily presumed that God created each and every species intact and for specific roles in the natural world, such thinking extended to thoughts such as: polar bears are white because God created them that way; cats purr because God created them that way; robins have red breasts because God created them that way.

We humans have a great need to explain the world around us by presuming that someone or something must have had it all figured out and planned out, we think that someone must have said, "We need robins with red breasts to fit herein the eco-system".

However, if the biologists are right, it does not work that way. Instead of jumping directly to robins with red breasts, we have instead an underlined process of evolution, which eventually produces robins with red breasts that appear to fit perfectly in the eco-system.

The beauty and functionality of the natural world springs from the success of its underlying processes and intricate mechanisms in a marvelous ticking clock manner.

History and the greatest of recorded works such as the Bible is filled with stories of Godlike visionaries who made great decisions, had great charisma, and led with great authority.

Fast forward a little and find yourself prior to the dramatic revolution in political thought of the 17th and 18th centuries, when the prosperity of a European kingdom or country for example, depended in large part on the quality of the King, and in case of England perhaps the Queen.

If you had a good King, then you had a good kingdom. If the King was a great and wise leader, then the kingdom might prosper.

However, if we compare the good King frame of reference with the approach taken at the founding of the United States, the critical question at the constitutional convention in 1787 was not "Who should be president?

"You are magnificent when you accept all of who you are without judgment"

Who should lead us? Who is the wisest among us? Who would be the best candidate? No, the founders of the United States concentrated on such questions as: "What processes can we create that will give us good presidents long after we are dead and gone? What type of enduring country do we want to build? On what principles? How should it operate? What guidelines and mechanisms should we construct that will give us that kind of country we envision?

Thomas Jefferson, James Madison, and John Adams were not charismatic visionary leaders in the "it all depends on me" mode of thinking, like a King or a Queen. No, they were organizational visionaries. They created a Constitution to which today, and all the future leaders would be guided by.

They focused on building a country. They rejected the good kingdom model. They took the architectural approach. They were clock builders!

However, notice that in the case of the United States, it is not a cold, mechanistic Newtonian or Darwinian clock; it is a clock based on human ideals and values. It is a clock built on human needs and aspirations.

It is a clock with spirit. In addition, that brings us to the second pillar of what is needed to be a visionary. Visionaries do not just build random clocks; they build particular types of clocks.

Although the shapes, sizes, mechanisms, styles, ages, and other attributes of the ticking clocks vary across visionaries, they all share an underlying set of fundamental characteristics.

Visionaries build clocks, they don't tell time.

The important thing to keep in mind is that once the shift from time telling, to clock building is made, what is required to become a visionary can be learned.

You do not have to accept the false view that until you are charismatic; you cannot become a visionary. There is no mysterious quality or elusive magic to be found in a visionary.

Indeed, once you learn the essentials, you can become a visionary. An essential step in becoming a visionary is to articulate a core ideology of what you stand for, and the values you cherish the most. A core ideology is the core values plus the purpose of your life.

The core values are the enduring tenants, a small set of general guiding principles of the fundamental reasons for your existence.

Also the real difference between success and failure in life can very often be traced to what we call beliefs, and the appeal beliefs have on our lives.

In order to survive and achieve success one must have a sound set of beliefs which to live by. The other important single factor in leading a successful life is faithful adherence to those beliefs.

Actions in accordance with our beliefs should always be altered if they are seen to violate fundamental Universal beliefs or Universal prime law. In most cases, a core value can be boiled down to a piercing simplicity that provides substantial guidance. A core value can be stated a number of different ways, yet it remains simple, clear, straightforward, and powerful.

"You are magnificent when you accept all of who you are without judgment"

Visionaries tend to have only a few core values. Values we would strive to live by for a hundred years regardless of changes in the external environment, even if the environment ceased to reward us for having these values, or perhaps even penalize us.

Conversely, which values would we be willing to change or discard if the environment no longer favored them?

One thing to keep in mind, core ideology does not come from mimicking the values of others, it does not come from following the dictates of outsiders; it does not come from reading books; and it does not come from a sterile intellectual exercise of calculating what values would be most pragmatic, most popular, or most profitable.

When articulating and codifying your core ideology, the essential step is to capture what is authentically believed, not what others set as their values that you should copy, or what the outside world thinks your ideology should be.

It is important to understand that your core ideology is an internal element, largely independent of external environments. To use an analogy, the founders of the United States didn't instill the core ideology of freedom and liberty because the environment dictate it, nor did they expect the country to ever abandon those basic ideals in response to environmental conditions.

They envisioned freedom and liberty as timeless ideals, independent of the environment.

"You are magnificent when you accept all of who you are without judgment"

The words: "We hold these truths to be self-evident," meant we hold these ideals to always work toward providing guidance, and inspiration to all future generations.

The same holds true in visionaries. In visionaries, the core values need no rational or external justification. Nor do they sway with the trends and fads of the day, or shift in response to changing conditions.

When it comes to purpose on the other hand, it is the set of fundamental reasons one exists beyond just living. A visionary finds his/her purpose by asking questions like: Why am I here? In other words, why do I exist? Purpose does not need to be unique, unlike core ideals; it is entirely possible that two people share a common or very similar purpose, just as it is entirely possible that two people can both share a rock-solid belief in the value "integrity".

The primary role of purpose is to guide and inspire you for the long haul, not necessarily to differentiate you from others.

When properly conceived, purpose is broad, fundamental, and enduring. A good purpose should serve to guide and inspire you for years; a century or more.

A visionary continually pursues but never fully achieves or completes his/her purpose, like chasing the horizon of the earth or pursuing a guiding star.

In short, a visionary can, and usually does, evolve into exciting new realities; yet remains guided by his/her core purpose.

Over time cultural norms change, goals change, competencies change, structures change, and reward systems change, but ultimately the only thing that should not change over time is your own unique core ideology.

Core ideology in a visionary works hand in hand with a relentless drive for progress that impels change and forward movement. The drive for progress is not sterile; the drive for progress is an internal force. The drive for progress does not wait for the external world to say: "It's time to change", "It's time to improve".

Like the drive inside a great artist or prolific inventor, it is simply there, pushing you outward and onward.

Through the drive for progress a visionary displays a powerful mix of self-confidence combined with self-criticism.

Self-confidence allows a visionary to set audacious goals and make bold and daring moves, sometimes flying in the face of conventional wisdom or prudence, it simply never occurs to a highly visionary person that it can't beat the odds, achieve great things, and become someone truly extraordinary.

Self-criticism on the other hand, pushes for self-induced change and improvement before the outside world imposes the need for change and improvement. It's what keeps you honest within yourself.

A visionary thereby becomes his/her own harshest constructive critic.

"You are magnificent when you accept all of who you are without judgment"

Although the core ideology and drive for progress usually trace their roots to specific individuals, a highly visionary person institutionalizes them, weaving them into the very fabric of who he/she is.

These elements do not exist solely as a prevailing ethos or culture. A visionary does not simply have some vague set of intentions or passion, it also has concrete, and tangible mechanisms to preserve his/her core ideology and to stimulate progress.

You discover your core ideology. Looking to the external environments does not derive it; you get it by looking inside. It has to be authentic.

You cannot fake an ideology. Nor can you just intellectualize it. Do not ask: What core values should I hold? Ask instead: What core values do I actually hold?

Core values and purpose must be passionate, and on a gut level or they are not core. The role of a core ideology is to guide and inspire you, not to differentiate; it is entirely possible that two people have the same core values or purpose.

It's not the content of the ideology that makes an individual a visionary, it's the authenticity, discipline, and consistency with which the ideology is lived, and the degree of alignment in actions in one's life that differentiates visionary individuals from the rest of the pack.

"You are magnificent when you accept all of who you are without judgment"

In other words, it is not what you believe that sets you apart; it is that you believe in something deeply, that you preserve it over time, and that you bring it to life with consistent alignment in all areas of your life. Ideology should not be confused with the concept of core competence.

Core competence is a concept that captures your capabilities, what you are particularly good at. Core ideology captures what you stand firm for, and why you exist.

Becoming a visionary requires you chart out both your core ideologies, and your core competence in your life, by continually holding yourself accountable and measuring your life's results, and the impact you have in the world around you.

Document it all on paper, make the effort to write your own story, much like a book… once you know what you want to write about, you can give it a title and every chapter supports the title. So too, your life is a book… ask yourself: What do I wish to fill the chapters of my book with? What is the title of my book? What is the purpose of my book? What impact do I want my book to have on the world?

Becoming a visionary requires you look within and identify your starting point of who you are right now. Knowing your starting point will ultimately allow you to navigate your life towards your desired direction.

"You are magnificent when you accept all of who you are without judgment"

Decide to win everyday

The following secret reveals several ideas that enable you to develop the mind of a winner. These ideas range from becoming your own hero to becoming a sexier more confident person. Once you develop the mind of a winner, you will be able to apply these ideas with self-assurance. By using these ideas consistently, you can win every day.

Is the idea of winning every day really possible, or is it just a mystical fantasy? Can you make every day a success so that each successful day culminates in a successful life? Or are you chained to failure each day, which culminates in an unsuccessful life? Each person's sense of life or their attitude toward life ultimately determines if he or she will win or lose every day.

How can you beat a negative attitude and the seemingly omnipresent upside-down world keeping you, and me from awakening the winning super hero. Is it really the external environment that impacts your ability to win?

Winning every day is an attitude.

That attitude arises from rational thinking. It does not arise from irrational, mystical thinking, from faith, praying, wishful thinking, or other similar concepts that spring from irrationalities.

Once you remove all the impurities from your mind and generate sufficient knowledge, success is practically guaranteed.

Moreover, that success is not temporary; it is permanent. With a clean, integrated thinking rational mind, you know that you will become a winner, permanently.

"You are magnificent when you accept all of who you are without judgment"

In reality, you will probably not win every single day of your life. That is because the law of averages holds that you will succeed and fail at various times in your life. That is okay.

The goal is to develop the attitude of seeking to win every day.

In other words, you want to approach each day as if you intend on succeeding and living the life of a winner. This secret provides you with unbeatable ideas you can use to win more often in every area of your life.

In baseball or football, everyone likes to see a home run or a one-hundred yard touchdown pass that wins the important ball games. However, almost no one likes to see the strenuous work that goes on during practice, and in the gym.

Yet, that extremely hard work in practice and in the gym provides the foundation for winners.

The home runs, and one-hundred yard touchdown passes are the results of hard work. Without that consistent daily effort such spectacular plays would be insignificant, let alone possible.

Winning teams do much more than perform a few glamorous plays. They win the tough little battles every day behind the scenes.

This secret integrates well with the mind of a winner. With this secret, you will see ordinary things in an entirely new light.

"You are magnificent when you accept all of who you are without judgment"

Areas such as time management, diet, and exercise that may have been problems for you in the past will now become opportunities to win every day. Also, you will see the idea of hero worship from a radically new perspective.

What is the result of these ideas?

You can feel better about your life on a day-to-day basis as well as from a long-range perspective. By winning every day, you grow in self-confidence, self-reliance, competence, and self-esteem. You become motivated to apply yourself one hundred per cent every single day.

You look forward to getting up each morning and living each day because you know how to win every day.

Are you ready to learn this secret to winning every day of your life?

Turn the page.

"You are magnificent when you accept all of who you are without judgment"

Be your own hero

The following are some assertions you might have heard while you were growing up, if not directly, you surely know of a friend that has experienced it.

"You will never amount to anything when you grow up!" "Who do you think you are? You can't do that!" "What's wrong with you; why can't you be like the other kids?" "Are you crazy? You are a dreamer; no one could ever do what you want to do!" "Can't you get anything right?"

Do any of these or similar assertions from adults to children sound familiar? Regardless of the intention of those who utter these remarks, the net result is the same in many cases.

The result is the diminishing of one's belief in one's own abilities and bright future. All such remarks either consciously or subconsciously undermine every child's natural exuberance, self-confidence, and self-esteem.

The undermining of every child's natural self-confidence and self-esteem is an inherent part of the upside-down world created by those who have profited from humanity's lack of knowledge of principles presented in this book. Why is essentially every child's self-confidence and self-esteem undermined?

So each child can be made a part of the upside-down world before he or she can understand what is happening. When each child becomes trapped in the upside-down world, which happens around six years of age, he or she will never know that another world exists. Thus, the upside-world can continue without opposition.

"You are magnificent when you accept all of who you are without judgment"

If an individual arises occasionally and sees beyond the upside-down world, he or she is simply murdered Socrates/Jesus/Giordano Bruno-style.

Through these dynamics, every person on planet Earth lives within the closed boundaries of an upside-down world. Moreover, these dynamics enable the corroded mind to rule everyone on the planet.

Some people have broken through the closed boundaries of the upside-down world. They have also left the corroded mind in the dust. How did they do this? They developed the mind of a winner, as discussed in the previous chapter.

That is the beginning of the end of the upside-down world. For, those with the mind of a winner will outflank and outcompete all corroded minds while they bring a right-side up world to planet Earth.

As entire populations shift from today's irrational world to tomorrow's rational world, children will be free eternally. They will not be drawn into an irrational world any longer. Additionally, they will no longer be bombarded by ludicrous concepts that spring from the corroded mind.

Children will remain clean, innocent, healthy, and powerful forever. Everyone else can recapture their childhood innocence, honesty, and genuine power for limitless prosperity, happiness, and love.

People throughout the world will transform from dependence to independence, and ultimately loving interdependence. As they do, they will be stunned by their new-found freedom.

"You are magnificent when you accept all of who you are without judgment"

That freedom will be all-pervasive; every aspect of their life will be marked by unbounded liberty. At first, people will not know what to do with such freedom. It will seem alien to them.

With the rise of the mind of a winner and a rational world, false authorities, and bogus leaders will become uncompetitive, even ridiculous.

Those external authorities, who survive by forcing others to sacrifice themselves, and their values, will not be able to survive.

They will become extinct. Against the newly emerging cosmic integrating minds of winners, external corroded authorities fade away like the oracle at Delphi.

Like the lost gods of antiquity, all such external authorities will vanish, never to return to planet Earth.

If highly touted leaders such as Odysseys, Alexander the Great, Julius Caesar, Pope Pius XII, and others fade along with their upside-world, who will people look up to? Who will people deem as heroes and model their own lives after?

In the forthcoming rational world, heroes will exist. In the upside-down world, those who are dangerous, even murderous, become heroes. For example, citizens believed Hitler to be a hero, as they did with Mao, Saddam Hussain, and other similar people.

"You are magnificent when you accept all of who you are without judgment"

Those who are productive, even magnanimous, become villains or "robber barons". For example, citizens believe John D. Rockefeller to be a villain, as they do Jay Gould and other similar people who contribute to the creation of jobs, markets, industries and who go against the norm of the upside-down world.

Those dynamics are reversed in the right-side up world. All who destroy human life, regardless of their good-sounding utterances, become villains. All who cause human life to flourish, regardless what envious people say about them, become heroes.

Thus, in the forthcoming rational world, anyone who objectively increases the quality of human life can become a hero.

Heroes can and do play a role in the development of your character. People look up to heroes as supreme examples of the greatness that is inherent in human beings. Heroes then influence and shape the lives of everyone they touch. Sometimes a hero can be one of your own family members, such as a virtuous parent or sibling.

Other times a hero can be a celebrity, such as a famous sports figure. Heroes can even come from fiction stories or movies, such as Superman.

The function of a hero remains the same, regardless if the hero is real or fictional. That function is to provide you with the inspiration to overcome your adversities, and achieve what you know is right and good. That is the contribution a hero makes to your life.

"You are magnificent when you accept all of who you are without judgment"

Super heroes exemplify great power, strength, courage, and ability. Beautiful heroes exemplify stunning physical beauty and alluring qualities.

Genius heroes exemplify startling brilliance, foresight, and mind power. The specific heroic traits that you admire are a personal choice. That is to say, you choose your own hero for purely personal reasons.

Having a hero is a natural, healthy part of conscious life, as long as you are free to choose your own hero, and that choice is made rationally.

Examples of childhood heroes are Batman and Robin, the Six Million Dollar Man, and Superwoman.

Examples of adult heroes are James Bond and Michael Jordan. Having a hero or several heroes can be a source of inspiration, fun, and excitement.

Heroes can also have a positive impact on your character development. For you might strive to cultivate those traits or virtues that you most desire in a hero. Again, a hero can be essentially any virtuous person, whether real or fictitious.

As you begin applying these secrets, something unique will occur. After cleansing your mind of its impurities, developing the mind of a winner, you will experience profound changes.

First, your outlook on life begins to shift. You see the endless losses that you endured are no losses at all.

"You are magnificent when you accept all of who you are without judgment"

Those losses from the upside-down world convert to gains in the right-side up world. Next, you begin to take on the character traits of super heroes. To your amazement, you begin to outcompete the super heroes.

Shortly, you discover that you can out-think, outflank, and outcompete anything in the upside-down world--including its heroes. So what can you do when, after developing the mind of a winner, you rise above even the super heroes?

You become your own hero. Does this sound like a radical idea? Maybe it is, but it is not mystical. So long as your thinking remains grounded in the facts of reality, you can be your own hero. Yes, with a few simple techniques, you can esteem your own person as much or more than the super heroes.

To become your own hero you need accurate self-knowledge. Illusions and distortions of facts will only result in long-term suffering. By fully understanding yourself and knowing your personal history, you are on an unshakable foundation.

Taking a character test will reveal your positive and negative traits. Such a test consists of asking yourself what strengths and weaknesses you have.

Then you can list those traits on paper in a side-by-side comparison, and you can clearly see your character development up to this point. You can see what traits you need to develop to strengthen your character.

Start by identifying your core ideologies, and your core competence, and then develop a character development plan of the super hero you strive to become.

"You are magnificent when you accept all of who you are without judgment"

This self-knowledge enables you to choose the direction you want to grow toward. You can then predict how your character will evolve in the coming years.

With this knowledge, you can shape yourself in the image of your ideal hero.

You can use your projected character development as your own hero. That hero is the future you. And, if chosen carefully, that hero can provide as much or more inspiration as any other known hero.

You create a situation that you control. That is to say, you decide which traits you want to develop, and you create an image of yourself already possessing such traits.

That image, regardless how far into the future he or she might be, becomes your source of inspiration. In short, that image becomes your hero. And that image is you, albeit in the future.

By becoming your own hero, everything you do works toward your own success. You put yourself in firm control of your own personal growth and character development.

You are no longer an outer-directed person; you are inner-directed by your core ideologies, and values.

That combination of being in control of your own character development and being inner-directed leads to genuine self-respect, self-esteem, and self-confidence.

You become happy to be alive when you become your own hero, and you work for your own success. This day-to-day happiness is the fuel that enables you to win every day.

"You are magnificent when you accept all of who you are without judgment"

Becoming an exceptional leader

Every leader should regularly take time to stop and ask themselves some important questions. Such as: Why do I do what I do? What do I stand for? What are my values? Why do they matter? What role do I play in helping others succeed? What is my contribution to the betterment of mankind within my own commitment to my own evolution and self realization?

Every leader needs to develop good character. One of my own icons of the ultimate example of leadership is King Solomon. King Solomon wrote:

"Keep thy heart with all diligence, for out of it are the issues of life".

In the Bible, the heart always refers to the seat of one's consciousness and emotions. The importance of character development was also underlined by arguably America's greatest leader, when George Washington declared: "Purity of morals is the only sure foundation of public happiness in any country."

Every leader needs to give importance to having and following through on his/her vision. King Solomon is credited with the famous saying: "Where there is no vision, the people perish."

When it comes to leadership, there are no truer words. Effective leaders, by definition, are leading people in a direction. Knowing what direction to take is vital. Communicating the importance and value of that direction is what leaders do when they cast the vision. It is crucial to understand the importance of vision.

"You are magnificent when you accept all of who you are without judgment"

Even when unclear as to the specifics, leaders work to keep people focused on the hope and aspirations of where they are headed and for what they are striving.

The most successful organizations are those whose people get behind the leader's vision voluntarily, and support it with all they have.

Someone has to set that vision in motion and keep it alive; that's the job of a good leader. Everything you do in life should come from a place within you to lead an organization.

Your family is an organization, your community is an organization, your city, state, country, company, and all around you is an organization seeking leadership. Your ability to develop self leadership is critical to not only your own success, but of the entire world.

Activating the real you requires you become a leader, more importantly a self leader.

"You are magnificent when you accept all of who you are without judgment"

Leaders invest in self knowledge and in developing wisdom

Knowledge and wisdom empowers a leader to be a beacon of human dignity among all those he/she influences. While you might get lucky in the lottery or an unexpected inheritance windfall, the truth is that most people will not acquire meaningful or stable happiness without wisdom. If you want to be a successful leader, you have to be knowledgeable and savvy, and invest in yourself by undertaking a system of knowledge.

Some call this spirituality, others call it self realization, the bottom line is that if you are not actively attached to a system that is focused on your higher self realization, you are doing yourself an injustice.

There are many systems out there. As for me the systems that I have embarked in have evolved, and has included Christianity, Masonry, Judaism, Kabbalah, and the Neothink Society. I have been fortunate to become a member of a global brotherhood of some forward thinkers who care about self realization as the means to enabling a better tomorrow for our children.

Whatever system works for you, take advantage of it fully, but be careful that it does not become dogmatic, when the system becomes dogmatic (meaning you feel compelled to do it out of fear), you've allowed irrationality to enter your mind, and such causes corrosion of your self-honesty.

"You are magnificent when you accept all of who you are without judgment"

Leadership requires perseverance

The theme of perseverance in the giants of history runs deep. You'll read in this book about Joseph the Righteous who was sold into slavery and later tempted to take short cuts to improve his life, but not succumbing to them, before finally getting the opportunity to govern Egypt and essentially be the vehicle for the survival of mankind at the time. Moses endured years in the desert, rejection by Pharoah, and then led the children of Israel – a frequently unruly lot – on a 40-year trek, before they could finally enter the Promised Land.

Consider the challenges and obstacles that confronted philosophers like Plato, Aristotle, Socrates and later the spiritual giants like R. Akiva, R. Shimon bar Yochai, and Jesus... all were murdered for standing by their character, character that has affected billions of lives for millenniums. These giants were self leaders, but they became such by first being good followers.

Perseverance is a critical skill of leadership. If you are not able to keep leading toward your goals when confronted with challenges and adversity, you will not succeed as a leader, let alone be an immortalized leader whose impact on the world will last for generations to come.

The path towards becoming a self leader is not easy, because it requires taking complete and full responsibility for your life, and as such you may be confronted with aspects of yourself that block you from becoming such a leader. The gift to you is that as you learn the character flaws you have, you can begin to reshape them and take control of them. Anything worth having is always met with great adversity.

"You are magnificent when you accept all of who you are without judgment"

Leadership requires an investment in self-realization

Mastering the skills of leadership requires that one begin with the qualities of a great leader, and those qualities of leadership can all be seen in the pages of the Bible which provide great insights about life, when you look beyond the religious values created around such insights.

A leader who exercises good moral character casts a vision, acquires knowledge, wisdom, and exemplifies perseverance; this will be a great leader indeed. You have to read beyond the simple stories of the Bible and beyond the dogma of religion to understand the powerful examples of these giants of the past.

How they stood true to their character, even in the face of death and how they were willing to give all they had for the sake of leading people out of their mediocre lives. A leader's goal is to set the example, and lead by example.

This requires that you first lead you. You must become someone lead by your core ideologies and core values, and you must project who the super hero of the future you will be, today. Day in and day out, be becoming that person.

"You are magnificent when you accept all of who you are without judgment"

Becoming a self leader

As you read this you may be asking, what about if I am not in a position of leadership yet? The hardest person to lead is your own self, to hold steadfast to your goals, and to have the discipline to go against the desire to relax, or even procrastinate. A leader is not defined by how many people work for him/her, a leader is defined by how many people his/her example influences, and in many cases the influence is not a direct one. For example if a friend comes to you with a problem he/she is facing, and it happens to be something you are struggling with yourself, leadership in that case isn't shown within the words of advise you give your friend, but by your commitment to take on that challenge and overcome it yourself with the consciousness that in doing so, you will make it possible for your friend to do so too.

This is the true essence of leadership. Taking on other's problems as your own, overcoming your own challenges as a means to helping others do the same. An exceptional leader is tuned in to his/her surroundings as a way to identify his/her areas of self improvement. What does this mean? For example, if someone that works for you just does not make it to meetings on time, is it possible there are areas in your own life where you don't show up on time? Perhaps you are supposed to have dinner with your family at 8:00pm but you work an extra 30 minutes and show up at home 30 minutes late. Most of us will use the excuse "I had to work another 30 minutes, the project needed me", but the family needed you too... so don't be surprised if employees show up 30 minutes late to work, or to an important meeting... because it is a reflection of you, and your lack of commitment to being on time in all aspects of your own life.

"You are magnificent when you accept all of who you are without judgment"

There is no such thing as separated work life and family life, what you do in one affects the other and this is true in all aspects of life.

Most leaders who don't realize this, end up hiring/firing many people and keep repeating the same patterns with the people they attract to the company, the truth is, the problem is not with the employee, the problem is buried deep inside the leader, and the only way to fix it, is to look within yourself, and fix yourself. When you do this, magically people show up on time, and so on. Yes, leaders are that powerful, if they learn how to harness that inner spirit that creates everything that resonates outside themselves.

Having a system of self realization for yourself, is more important that an MBA, or any other educational investment you can make. If you look at the most exceptional leaders of all time, some of them never went to College, but all of them left behind inspiration, because they understood the greatest secret of leadership of all time: Self realization through a path of self realization, or as some call it spirituality.

Becoming a self leader is about becoming inner self directed; beings of emanation of positive attributes that contribute to the betterment of humanity, therefore the most important person to lead, first and foremost is your own self and this is accomplished every time the desire to take is transformed into the desire to give. Leadership is about giving a lot more than being served by others, therefore to become an exceptional leader, one must become an exceptional servant. We are not talking about altruism here; we are talking about creating for others that which one wishes to experience him/herself.

"You are magnificent when you accept all of who you are without judgment"

When you care deeply about the people that voluntarily get behind your vision, be it your family, friends, employees, peers, and others, and when you personally take them under your wing, you begin to act within yourself accordingly, and you transform within yourself the very thing that those you lead lack.

Any lack you identify outside of yourself is simply a reflection of something you need to become better at yourself. You must lead yourself out of chaos in order to remove chaos from other people's lives.

Next time you are bothered by someone's behavior or actions, know that the only reason it bothers you is because you possess that character flaw within yourself, otherwise you would not notice it in them.

To improve the world, to make the world a better place, you must lead the world out of chaos; the first person to lead is yourself out of your own chaos.

That's where exceptional leadership starts.

Within you, within me.

"You are magnificent when you accept all of who you are without judgment"

We can learn about leadership from a man that lived over 3000 years ago

You may have heard, or read the story of Joseph the Righteous, the son of Jacob the Patriarch. We can apply principles to live by, from the giants that have been immortalized before us.

Joseph the Righteous is the story of every living human being on earth - the struggle, the fight, to reveal the highest version of self that will benefit thousands, if not millions, or billions of people.

Let's review the story together:

(1) Joseph the Righteous was sold by his brothers as a slave and was ultimately purchased by Potiphar.

(2) His master, Potiphar eventually recognized Joseph's abilities and appointed him as a leader over his entire household

(3) Potiphar's wife attempted to seduce Joseph, but he did not succumb.

There are three major lessons for self leaders within these Biblical "metaphorical" references. I am going to go into more details but as a summary they are:

"You are magnificent when you accept all of who you are without judgment"

(1) The importance of turning your mis-fortunes into your greatest lifelong values and assets.

(2) Knowing that all you are capable of, is not your own, but rather a Consciousness that is pervasive within everyone. You just happen to be the one to have the gift to share it... nothing more. It does not make you better or smarter, actually what it does, it makes you more responsible in giving more to others. Recognizing this principle is what separates the creator/giver, with the created/taker. The self leader, with those needing to be lead.

(3) While short cuts and one time blasts seem so alluring, there are no short cuts in achieving your values and activating your higher self, awakening the real you takes work, perseverance, integrated thoughts followed by integrated actions, patience, desire and the willingness to do whatever it takes to share your gifts and talents to contribute to the advancement of society, as the means for achieving your own highest values.

A good leader has to be self directed by his/her inner higher self - not for the sake of morals, or ethics, but for the sake of self maturity and character development to awaken the higher self. The higher self is not ego driven; it is driven by love for others, which starts by loving oneself.

Loving oneself requires self honesty, and acceptance, and an effort to become complete within, because all we see outside of ourselves is what is within ourselves... what you see, is what you are, so if you don't like what you see, change who you are.

"You are magnificent when you accept all of who you are without judgment"

One of Joseph's talents was the preternatural ability to interpret dreams, and he never attributed this extraordinary capability to his own efforts.

An effective leader must be self-confident and sure of himself or herself without arrogance. Joseph knew of his abilities to interpret dreams, but he was modest and did not desire to take credit for his abilities. An amazing value of great leaders is modesty/humility, and being able to be lead by others and open to learn from others.

Aristotle said that a great leader must first be one who has been lead.

Joseph's brothers had wronged him in the most horrible way imaginable: they sold him as a slave out of envy for Joseph's gifts. Joseph was sold at the age of 17 and toiled as a slave for almost two decades. He had the opportunity to get even, and could easily have justified it, but Joseph had no interest in vengeance, so when the time came, he took all of his misfortunes and turned them into the greatest of assets, and in fact he not only was responsible for the survival of his family during 7 years of famine, but that of the entire world... He became, as is written "Master of the World".

Sometimes the people you trust in your life, betray you, straight up go out of their way to hurt you... but then something amazing happens, you reach a point in life where you see all those things as your greatest assets, bringing you exactly where you need to be with the skills and the power to become something you could not have become, unless you had experienced those challenges. The movie Slum dog Millionaire is an amazing example of this concept. See it if you have not.

We don't spend enough time being present without judgment, and this causes us to miss how an otherwise difficult situation is actually leading us towards bliss in the future. It is only difficult because we refuse to be present without judgment, because we refuse to practice acceptance.

"You are magnificent when you accept all of who you are without judgment"

Being present and practicing acceptance allows you to begin to see problems as nothing more than tasks the Universe gives you to become the best version of you, challenges that help you unblock the real you within you; even more amazing is that you begin to see that you created those challenges (conscious of it or not) to help you become who you are meant to be. The goal is to see them this way not after they happen, but while they are happening so that you can shift from victim to creator consciousness.

A good leader is not concerned with avenging slights to his or her honor (aka the ego). Rather, he/she cares about what is best for everyone, and will overlook personal slights. Individuals who spend their days trying to get even are not suitable as leaders. The best leader is one who looks for ways to serve others, to help others succeed. The ultimate leader is the one who leads, and also works to enable everyone around him/her to personally succeed, the later being the most important attribute.

No matter how good you are at something, even if you have the gift as Joseph the Righteous to see the future, recognize that this isn't something that is yours, you are simple a channel. Just like a mobile phone uses radio waves that have existed before the invention of mobile phones... the mobile phone is a device that taps into, and activates the radio waves already in existence, but it does not generate the radio waves.

You and I are devices that can be calibrated to tap into, and activate other waves already in existence, waves that generate every conceivable fulfillment we desire. So no matter how successful we are at anything, we must always remember we are just like the mobile phone, using what is available (the radio waves), that we did not create, the ever expanding Universal Consciousness, to channel those energy sequences (waves) to others through ourselves.

"You are magnificent when you accept all of who you are without judgment"

This humble mind set will enable our ability to channel more and more, much like Joseph the Righteous we begin to see that all of our experiences and gifts are not for our own consumption, but rather they come because of our willingness to create value for others.

Sometimes we get tempted with short cuts, a little white lie that can help close the deal, an underhanded business deal, an alluring offer for short term gains, and so on; we must remember that when Potiphar's wife, tried to seduce Joseph, no written law (moral or ethical) existed at that time against him sleeping with her. Joseph was inner-directed by his connection to Universal Consciousness and knew that his entire fulfillment would come in due time, without the need for short cuts, or one shot blasts of gratification.

Imagine, here is a man suffering for almost two decades, and a sexy powerful woman, who could open so many doors for him, offers him pleasure and he says no?

When something comes easy, beware, it may be the thing that could make you miss out on becoming "Master of the World", sort of speak. When you look into the stories of entrepreneurs like Walt Disney, BF Goodridge and others, some of these men spent years in jail, had many bankruptcies, and had many challenges pursuing their dreams, much like Joseph some spend almost two decades in despair but ultimately created so much value for other people, that they will forever be immortalized.

I mean Disney created a vehicle for people to feel happy. Who doesn't want to be happy? Yet it took several bankruptcies and difficulties to create that value for others. Leaders don't give up, they just keep pushing forward, their beliefs and commitment to improve the life of others, drives them to push through all kinds of adversity. Overcoming adversity is the key to happiness, it's not the end result, it is the challenge that creates happiness.

"You are magnificent when you accept all of who you are without judgment"

As leaders, there are three principles we can take away from the story of Joseph the Righteous, (there are many other codes behind the story and the Gematria of the name and writings, stand for something much grander... but for the sake of this topic we'll stick to three that apply in life).

(1) Don't look at challenges as nothing more than tasks you need to work through that will lead to unlocking your inner higher self, the real you is like a pearl undergoing friction before it becomes a valuable precious gem.

(2) Be humble in your success, arrogance stops the connection to the Universal Consciousness that holds the blissful fulfillment of all you desire. Do everything with love, and interest in creating value for others, not for the sake of validation from others, or altruism but because doing so is the secret to living a happy fulfilling life.

(3) Persistence, integrated thoughts, and integrated actions will create long lasting fulfilling results - short cuts, as tempting as they may be, simply push away unlocking your fullest potential, or worse feed into the illusion that you are succeeding, till you have a rude awakening.

About short cuts, they do work for a while, and then the pain of starting over is far greater than the pain of just saying no to the short cut in the first place (this is not just something I know, it is something I have lived). One way or the other, we live in a time today where each of us, has to fulfill his/her fullest potential. To awaken the need to let go who we have been, and become who we are meant to be, who we really are; one soul, one mind, one Consciousness centered on unity and love, to create a reality based on values for each other. That reality already exists; we just need to live it. More on this topic later in the book.

"You are magnificent when you accept all of who you are without judgment"

With the global financial crises we are in, the story of Joseph the Righteous is about us, our need to overlook the wrongs we've experienced in life and lovingly fulfill our unique role to add value in advancing humanity towards peace, prosperity and total blissful fulfillment; which already exists just like the radio waves, all we need to do is whatever it takes to transform, tap into it, and activate it in our lives.

When we do that, we won't even need a mobile phone device to use radio waves and communicate across distances; we will activate that ability within.

Yes the real you and I, inside you and me, are that powerful. Imagine the power to overcome and change anything and everything, which is what Joseph the Righteous is all about.

The story of Joseph the Righteous is about being present at all times without judgment, accepting one's role in life while not fully comprehending along the way what that role is, but knowing with complete certainty that that role will be fulfilled in due time, even if the challenges along the way seem to make us feel like we have fallen off track.

The bigger picture

Most people do not integrate their work with their life. Many people despise their work, they cannot wait for the weekend, and they dread the arrival of Monday.

Most people today get their sense of self-esteem, self-worth, and identity from what they do in their spare time versus what they do in their career while producing values.

This sad and unfortunate limitation encourages the default to laziness and dishonesty, which in turn frequently leads to alcohol, drug use, and neurosis.

Such people nonthinkingly turn to external sources such as alcohol, drugs, happy hour, parties, spectator sports, and hobbies in order to get short "one-shot" blasts of self-esteem, joy, pleasure, and happiness.

These one-shot blasts are un-integrated so they do not last; they do not contribute to one's net long term happiness -- one's happiness bank account.

Still, in order to feel "good", or to feel "happy", people are driven to continually seek one-shot blasts. This usually leads to a life of wasted superfluous activities, alcohol and drug use, poor health, and very limited genuine self-esteem and happiness.

For indeed, how much honest self-esteem can be earned from one-shot blasts? How much genuine pride and self-esteem can be earned by being the world's best sports fan? Or by being the best television watcher?

"You are magnificent when you accept all of who you are without judgment"

Or by being the best drinker? One need only take the activity to its maximum achievement-capacity conclusion to see its honest value. It then becomes obvious, for example, that being the best at watching television, or the best sports fan, or the best drinker is of little or no value to long term self development.

However, being the best in one's career will lead to great values for yourself, and society.

All genuine happiness is derived through the creation of values. To not continually build, and exchange values is to default to the lazy, self-lie norms promoted by today's upside-down world.

Defaulting in the areas of value creation, and self-honesty closes the door to all future growth. It is crucial to begin orienting your life around the creation of values as opposed to trying to find happiness from external sources. Your happiness must develop, and grow from within yourself.

All self-developed skills grow with time, and use. Every person can capture a life of productive value creation to earn ever increasing prosperity, happiness, and love.

"You are magnificent when you accept all of who you are without judgment"

Wealth and happiness

What is the relationship between money and happiness? Is money a cause, and happiness an effect? Or is money evil, and a hindrance to happiness? Most people have heard contradictory assertions about money, ranging from "money makes people happier" to "money is the root of all evil." Upon close examination, one can see the relationship between the two. Moreover, one can see the primary role of wealth.

Money is a medium of exchange for values.

A person produces values, and exchanges those values for money. The more values one produces and exchanges with others, the more money he or she can accumulate.

Then the person can use this money to produce more values, and purchase values from others.

This is a simplified explanation of wealth production. What about happiness? Happiness is an effect, but money is not the cause, at least not the primary cause. The cause of happiness is the achievement of one's core ideologies, and core values.

For example, say a person consciously values an enriching love relationship. That person then prepares herself to experience such a relationship. Later, she meets a man that she admires and they initiate a relationship.

That relationship then develops into a growing love relationship. She may not explicitly grasp the dynamics involved, but she feels happy.

"You are magnificent when you accept all of who you are without judgment"

Happiness is an effect. The cause is achieving one's values. This presumes that a person has chosen a hierarchy of values. If a person holds money as a high value and earns it, he or she will experience happiness.

The same is true of all values, such as self-esteem, romantic love, and aesthetic pleasures.

Ultimately, however, happiness along with prosperity, and romantic love, depends on one fundamental condition.

Without this condition, one will not experience abiding happiness, prosperity, or romantic love. What is that condition?

That condition is "measurable productive accountability".

No matter how much money or material abundance one might have, productive work is essential to one's happiness. Even if a person wins a billion dollar lottery, that person would need to engage in measurable productive accountable activities to experience abiding happiness.

Why would even a billionaire need to engage in measurable productive accountable activities to achieve abiding happiness?

Wouldn't that billionaire be able to buy his way to happiness? Wouldn't that person derive happiness from the unlimited consumption of material goods?

The reason every adult human being needs to engage in measureable productive accountable work is for physical and psychological survival. One does not work for higher causes or altruistic reasons or duty to one's family, religion, or nation.

"You are magnificent when you accept all of who you are without judgment"

One does not engage in productive work because of tacit or expressed obligations to others. The only reason one engages in productive work is for one's own physical and psychological survival.

In the case of the billionaire, or any individual who is financially independent, he or she still needs to work. In this situation, the individual no longer works for physical survival.

The individual's material needs are already taken care of. He or she works for psychological survival.

Only productive work can deliver the self-esteem that is needed for psychological survival. Sexual conquests cannot deliver the self-esteem needed for psychological survival. Neither can praying, hobbies, manipulating others, drug use, criminal scores, killing, or any other activity. In the long run, the avoidance of productive work leads to the subconscious thought, "I wish I was dead."

Measurable productive accountable work is the foundation of happiness. It is also the foundation of prosperity. Productive work is indispensable to human beings.

Producing more values than one consumes is the essence of a measurable productive accountable and happy life.

Equally important is that no one can dictate to others what work to engage in. For some people's productive work might consist of landscaping, painting, composing music, or writing. For others, these may simply be hobbies.

"You are magnificent when you accept all of who you are without judgment"

Others might choose teaching, healing, or engineering as their means of productive work.

The guiding principle here is that productive work requires a long-range perspective, rational goals, a focused mind, and consistent effort.

In other words, one needs to approach productive work rationally to experience abiding prosperity and happiness. One can apply this principle to all productive work, including janitorial work, sales, artwork, building a business, or any other productive activity.

If productive work is the foundation for all abiding happiness and earned prosperity, and essentially everyone wants to be happy and prosperous, why doesn't everyone engage in productive work? There is a two-part answer to this question.

The first part deals with a deeply personal matter. That personal matter is a choice every human being on the planet has to make. Each person has to make the choice to exert the consistent high effort that productive work demands. In essence, each individual human being has to make the following choice: to exert consistent high effort or default to laziness. And that choice has to be made every day by every human being.

The second part of the answer is a cultural issue. The culture in the upside-down world cleverly works to foster laziness, incompetence, and criminal thinking.

I call it the Paris Hilton syndrome, everyone wants to live like a billionaire without earning it, and just have a good old time consuming more than is produced. This unfortunately does not create self happiness for the long haul.

In other words, the culture subtly spreads a dependency attitude in the minds of people. As people absorb this cleverly promoted attitude throughout their life, they subconsciously accept it.

People begin to think it is "cool" to take it easy, sit back, and let others do the work. Those who exert the constant high effort needed for value production are labeled as uncool, overachievers, workaholics, or other disparaging names.

Some of those consistent hard workers are attacked, thrown into jail, and destroyed. Attacked for working hard to produce objective values? Thrown into jail for delivering goods, and services that everyone's life depends on? How could that be?

Such are the dynamics that comprise the upside-down world.

By developing the mind of a winner, you will wield genuine power. With genuine power, you will leave that ridiculous world behind forever. You will eliminate floundering, perpetual truth seeking, endless losses, and unbearable psychological, and emotional pain.

Also, for the first time on planet Earth, forced poverty will become obsolete. Every person who develops the mind of a winner inevitably prospers without limits. For, each such person steps out of a stagnant irrational world and steps into a dynamic rational world.

Yes, by developing the mind of a winner, you too can say good-bye to the upside-down world.

"You are magnificent when you accept all of who you are without judgment"

Furthermore, you can say hello to limitless wealth, profound happiness, and excitement for the rest of your life.

With the mind of the winner, described in an earlier chapter, is the honest integrating mind that can generate happiness without limits. You can, with that rational mind, understand everything you need to know for unlimited bliss in your life.

The days of thinking, "That's over my head" or "I can't understand that" are numbered.

The honest heroic and self lead master mind can understand anything in existence.

"You are magnificent when you accept all of who you are without judgment"

Letting go of fear

Have you ever heard yourself saying: "There must be another way to go through life besides being pulled through it kicking and screaming"? I have learned that we can overcome our bouts of depression, guilt and anger by finally recognizing the source of our feelings and gaining control of life's outcomes. Finding love for life, or love in life however, requires a willingness to change, and transform.

Most of us want to rid ourselves of pain and frustration and experience peace of mind, love and fulfillment in life, at the same time we want to control, predict future events, and maintain our old self-concepts. In other words, we do the same things over and over, and expect different results. Some say that is the sign of insanity or stupidity, however to most people that is simply what life is, ups and downs, and a series of twists and turns much like a roller coaster.

To many people life is like a casino; a daily rolling of the dice and winning is a very complicated feat, while losing is just part of the game. No wonder we consequently resist any real change, and continue to feel isolated and unloved, or worse unfulfilled altogether. We have been conditioned to believe that life is a casino with the odds stacked up against us.

What you are about to read from here on out, are not new ideas, but the knowledge was kept a secret for many years, because most people weren't ready to accept it, and many were put to death for trying to teach it, including Jesus, who understood these concepts better than any other being that has ever walked the earth.

"You are magnificent when you accept all of who you are without judgment"

Why was it secret? Think about the technology advancements we've had in the past 100 years. If I told you 200 years ago that you could walk into a room and turn on a switch and a light would come on, you would think I was a witch. If I told you 100 years ago we could talk on a device with other people across the world using radio waves that have existed in the Universe forever, you would think I was crazy.

Similarly, right now, as you read this, thousands of signals are coming across your very eyes; radio signals, TV station signals, wireless phone conversations, etc. You can't see them, but you don't doubt they are there, you know they are there. Why can't you see them or hear them? You need electronic devices to tap into them.

Similarly, the Universe is full of signals, called energy sequences of love, health, and fulfillment; why is it we can't see them, or hear them or feel them all the time? How do we tap into them? What is the device we need to receive this kind of signal? Does the device exist?

The device is your consciousness. What is consciousness? Consciousness is the real you. The real you is a thought in action.

Yes, you are the materialized version of a thought, and therefore the real you is your consciousness. Fear is your biggest enemy in achieving your truest potential in the reality of actions. The reality of action is the material existence we experience with our five senses, our intellect and our logic.

Fear creates space between illusions and reality, the more fear the more the illusion of being separated, the more lack of love we feel in our lives and the more unfulfilled. Separated from what you may ask? We'll discuss this later on in the book.

"You are magnificent when you accept all of who you are without judgment"

Fear works to victimize us and to immobilize us from taking action in our lives and push us into contemplation, procrastination, and a never ending cycle that is self feeding for the purpose of eliminating any possibility for fulfillment, love, happiness, security, success and purpose in our life.

We can dissolve fear by sharing, giving, seeking the best in others, going against our negative nature, and restricting our egotistic nature. Ultimately it can all be summed up as "transforming into our true selves", instead of living in the illusion of our bodies.

What is real? Too often we accept feedback from our physical senses as the only reality. However, love, though intangible, is real, and so is fear that frequently thwarts love.

Our minds constantly replay all our memories like a video. Included are tons of distorted obsolete guilt and fears, which squeeze out the joy of the present. Worse, our mind convinces us that all fear is a result of our upbringing, social economic environment, and so on. Our mind is constantly convincing us to blame everything around us as a way to transfer blame and not take responsibility for ourselves.

Our mind is a slave to the physical realm we think is our only reality; therefore we think we can solve all of our problems in the existence of our body, in the physical dimension of ourselves, instead of our consciousness.

Which part of our mind does this? What is the difference?

"You are magnificent when you accept all of who you are without judgment"

Allow me to explain by asking you: Where do your desires originate? Does our brain create desire? Can you buy, touch desire? Is it physical?

Desires come from our consciousness, and we manifest them physically. However not all of our desires are manifested. Why?

We desire love, and yet we often just get used. We desire wealth and yet often we fail at the last minute, and feel like we are cursed. We desire health, and yet we can't seem to get to the gym. We desire happiness and yet we just can't seem to hold on to it long enough.

Why is it so difficult?

Think of yourself as being energy, and channeling energy towards you and away from you. Now think of your car's antenna, it picks up the radio signal as long as it isn't blocked by too much concrete.

You get in a parking lot underground and your signal is gone. Why? Because your signal is now being blocked. We have an antenna too, and we block the signals that are out there. Love, happiness, fulfillment; we can't seem to receive them. Why?

Fear. Fear is the opposite of love. Fear is the root of all evil, and for thousands of years establishments have used fear to control the masses, such fear has caused separation between us, such fear has caused us to become dishonest with ourselves by trying to live by standards put in place by those who have desired to control you and me.

Fear blocks the real you from living a chaos free life.

"You are magnificent when you accept all of who you are without judgment"

Love and fulfillment starts after we let go of fear

Even in the present, our priorities frequently become scattered, and filled with conflict as we try to juggle too much at once. But by choosing a single life's goal, that of emanating all we wish to experience from within outwardly, we become better able to focus our energies and we remove the blockages that don't allow us to tap into the Universal bliss producing signals that are all around us.

Our five senses limit our realities; our supernal senses enable us to feel love, and fulfillment in our lives. All the negativity surrounding us comes from our limited five senses. Our supernal senses are still within ourselves, more on this later in the book.

Judging people, for example comes natural because it is a byproduct of our five senses, and a manifestation of how our five senses, which include emotions and intellect, limit us and hold us slaves to our illusions. Judgment causes fear to exist.

On the flip side, it's more difficult to love people, especially those who try to hurt you. Jesus said, and I paraphrase "What good is in loving those that love you? Where's the gain in that? Love your enemies as you love yourself".

What did he mean by this? What lesson was he trying to teach us? If we start by loving and forgiving people, vs. judging them, it will become more and more apparent that other people do not have to change for us to experience love, peace, and fulfillment.

"You are magnificent when you accept all of who you are without judgment"

This point begs a question, what is forgiveness? Forgiveness isn't what we perceive with our limited five senses, it isn't what religion teaches that we empower ourselves in such a way that we forgive other's wrong doing.

What makes us better than the person we forgive? What empowers us to forgive them, as we know forgiveness to be?

Here lies the secret in Jesus' words. Forgiveness is about taking responsibility for our feelings, our reaction to how others may have wronged us; forgiveness is removing the blame for our own feelings from others. It is no longer blaming another person for our own reactions; it is about taking responsibility for ourselves and our reactions, it is about recognizing in ourselves the opportunities for improvements, it is realizing that others who push our buttons are actually performing a great thing for our own good.

When you look into a mirror and you see a scar, do you blame the mirror? Do you say, I hate you mirror for causing the scar? All the mirror has done is given you a chance to see what is part of you, the mirror is just the messenger. Often people who seem to wrong us, push our buttons, challenge us, they are messengers trying to help us recognize where we need to transform.

What bothers us about others is true about our own selves. Towards the end of this book, I will reveal a profound secret to living a chaos free life and why we are bothered by other's actions at a much deeper level, for now keep reading.

"You are magnificent when you accept all of who you are without judgment"

We will also discuss the role free will has in living a chaos free life, for now I want you to ask yourself: Do I chose to find love or find faults? Do I choose to be a love giver or a love seeker? Do I chose to be alone, or do I choose to find my soul-mate? Do I seek my happiness, or do I push it away? Do I see things for what they are, or do I see things for what I'd like to believe they are?

We are what we believe. We are always either expressing love or fear. Fear and love can never be experienced at the same time. By choosing love more often than fear, we can change the nature and quality of our relationships and our lives.

What we experience in life is limited only by what we can give. So it's not a question of, why am I not lucky? Why can't I have it all? If we ask, it is because our consciousness is telling us that those areas of our lives are the areas we are not actively putting out ourselves, it means we are not actively contributing to the luck of others, and to the well being of others.

Perhaps we don't give to the poor, or we don't help a friend who's jobless by making introduction to people we know could help them or perhaps we don't help our co-workers be successful because we are too busy worrying about our own ladder climbing efforts, and position.

Our conscious real questions should be what can I do to create luck? What can I do to have it all? However, our fears take these proactive thoughts and translated them for us into questions of limitations; they force us into a reactive way of thinking. It is a constant struggle inside of us. But we can learn to recognize it, and transform.

"You are magnificent when you accept all of who you are without judgment"

We are often mistaken by thinking that we can give anyone anything other than what we want for ourselves. A man once asked Mother Theresa if he could fly with her on her way to Mexico City to discover inner peace, with a gentle smile, she replied "I would have no objection about your joining me, but since you said you wanted to learn about inner peace, I think you would learn more about inner peace if you would find out how much it costs to fly to Mexico City and back, and give that money to the poor". What a powerful lesson in giving, and receiving.

In order to receive, we must first give. In order to be loved, we must first love; in order to be rich we must first enrich others. Our ability to find love or anything we desire is in our ability to create an opportunity for such a thing to enter our lives. We create luck, we create love, we create happiness, we create peace, we do it all by emanating it with others first.

Next time you blame your mother, father, upbringing, your job, your wife, husband, your children for your problems, think: Is it my fears excusing me from taking responsibility for where I am so I don't have to do anything about it? Am I really just trying to avoid the real work I have to do to overcome the problems I have. Is the past just a way to excuse the work I need to do towards the future?

We talked about forgiveness earlier; practicing forgiveness is a very powerful way to raise our consciousness and remove fear from our lives, the more we learn to take responsibility for our own outcomes in life, the higher our consciousness, the higher our consciousness the less chaos in our lives. The chaos just doesn't manifest in our own lives anymore.

"You are magnificent when you accept all of who you are without judgment"

Simply put, life is not what you think life is, life is what you think of life. What you think is what motivates your actions, and your actions generate your moods.

Lack of willingness to forgive creates a bitter mixture of distorted perceptions. Holding grievances or speaking condemning words doesn't help anyone; it only brings more bitterness. However, forgiveness opens new doors in our hearts. Neither guilt nor innocence or ethics or religion should play a part in practicing forgiveness. Forgiveness is all about taking responsibility for ourselves.

A businessman once consciously determined to bury his long-kept anger over a client's unpaid bill, informing his client that no more bills would be sent. Surprisingly, the man paid the money, and the business man gave it to someone who was in real need. Thus, by the vehicle of forgiveness, many hearts were healed.

The businessman forgave (released his client from the responsibility of his own anger) and took responsibility for his feelings. Only when the businessman was able to change his own attitude, did he open the way for that bill to be paid, and he opened another opportunity for himself by sharing that money with others, thus creating a counter cycle to fear and opening more gateways to fulfillment, and love in his life. The businessman created circuitry, and his actions had a quantum effect on several lives.

Now let's talk about anger. We are never upset for the reason we think we are upset. It is easy to presume that the outside world is the cause and we are the effect. But this thinking is backwards. The world doesn't cause feelings, just as that client did not really cause the businessman's' anger. Peace of mind begins with our own thoughts, and extends outward, so can anger.

"You are magnificent when you accept all of who you are without judgment"

Remember what we discussed? We draw energy and put it outward? What we wish outward is what we draw inward to our own selves.

All negative feelings (jealousy, anger, resentment, etc) in reality represent some form of fear, and fear frequently triggers other problems. Back pain is sometimes a manifestation of harbored hatred or envy, for instance, so whenever you are tempted to be fearful, remind yourself that you can experience love instead.

A fearful past will extend into a fearful future making us feel vulnerable, and out of control. This cycle of fear holds the assumption that anger occurs because we have been attacked. It also assumes that counterattack is justified. But we can choose to be robots of our five senses, or be free to follow our inner guidance, and respond with understanding and love.

Think of a doctor that is put into a position of saving a tubercular woman's life by giving her mouth-to-mouth resuscitation. If that doctor chooses to feel like he is attacked by his patients and lives in fear of catching the dreaded disease, the patient will likely die. If the doctor chooses to save the woman's life, and consequently nothing happens to the doctor, it dawns on him that he has just learned a great lesson. The lesson is that when we are totally absorbed in giving, we feel no fear and often we become immune to all kinds of problems, including illness.

I chose the word "attacked", and you may say that the patient wasn't attacking the doctor, however this is exactly what our fears do, they make us feel like we are under attack. Fears attack us and pummel us into submission by creating the illusion that everything is happening to us.

"You are magnificent when you accept all of who you are without judgment"

The attacks originate in the mind, therefore we want to transform our thinking and replace thoughts that others want to hurt us with thoughts of love. To achieve inner peace, and love in our lives, we must perceive a world where everyone is innocent. We can do this by changing our minds about what we see, by choosing to see the good in others, by finding their God like personalities.

Often, as we go through life's maturing process, we also tend to learn the art of distrust. We become paranoid of life itself, not to mention distrustful of others (work associates, sales clerks, car dealers, spouses, children, partners, etc.) But when we let go of this sense of "victimization", then our relationships become based on genuine respect and love.

A fifteen year old boy, whose head was run over twice by a tractor, was left blind and paralyzed. How did he maintain his optimism? He looked for the positive in everyone, and paid no attention to the negative things, he refused to believe in the word impossible. This boy refused to feel sorry for himself. He could feel that the world had dealt him a blow; however he chose to see the good in it by becoming a miracle in other people's lives, simply by his attitude and take life by the horns demeanor.

This example shows how we can rise above the limitations of our five senses, this boy could not see (visually) and yet his vision of reality was stronger than ever. Sometimes we have eyes, but we do not see, because we chose to be blinded by our illusions.

"You are magnificent when you accept all of who you are without judgment"

We have the tools, but don't use them correctly. We chose to be deaf and blind and go through life this way. Imagine going into a dark room, and having to walk across the room with many obstacles. Will you make it across without bumping into something, without pain?

Imagine being in that room, and all you have to do is turn on the light switch so you can see and avoid the obstacles. Just because you are in a dark room, and no one told you that there is light there, it does not mean you should not look for the light switch in that room, before walking through it.

Life is the same, the Light is there, we often are blinded by the fact that we've been told that to deal with obstacles, and pain is normal, we watch others go through life as if in a dark room, and we do the same.

Whose fault is it that we do the same?

The Light is there, we just chose the easy thing to do; follow, instead of being self leaders and asking: Where is the light switch?

Becoming a self leader, and taking full accountability for yourself, affords you to ask questions you would otherwise not ask. It allows you to challenge everything, and opens you to find solutions to otherwise difficult situations.

We have done the same things over and over for thousands of years, with the same failures. It does not have to be that way.

"You are magnificent when you accept all of who you are without judgment"

Succeeding in life is much like the game of golf

In the game of golf, the only competition you face is yourself. You practice, and work hard at removing bad habits on how you grip the club, your stance, your club strategy, and your swing. The greatest golfer does not analyze how another golfer plays, he/she works on improving his/her own game by developing consistent habits that generate consistent good results. There is an amazing lesson to be learned from the game of golf in life.

Many people spend a great deal of time, figuring out how to become better than others, but there is a fundamental problem with this strategy. The problem is that you are essentially competing within a zero sum strategy, you are competing for your slice of the pie, and there is only so much to go around, so you end up forcing someone out of the game, and ultimately the same might happen to you. It's not a true win win strategy, it's limited.

What's the alternative?

Creating value means adding something to the pie that is missing... making the pie bigger, this not only benefits you, but others too, which means as they also add to the pie, you benefit again because the pie just got bigger for everyone, which includes you. Success happens within you, meaning that you focus on developing yourself to be consistent, productive, resilient, and above all someone that adds value, vs. takes value from others to add to the self.

The real competition is in beating the desire to compete with everything external of you, and using how well you do that as the yardstick metrics of your success.

The only thing holding you back from growing is internal lack of focus, vision, and core ideology. Ask yourself: What do I stand for, and how does it add value to others?

When we are in creator mode, anything can be accomplished, when we go into taker mode, everything goes downhill from there. This economic crash we have recently experienced is a testament of what happens when we consume more than we produce, when we take more than we give. All of us caused it; the only way out of it, and the only way for it to never happen again, is to become beings of creative and giving forces, vs. beings that need stuff to be happy.

This crash has come from the need to compete in a zero sum proposition world. If you are not actively adding value, you are taking from the pie and eventually this causes recessions, and depressions. The key ingredient to growing as an individual is much like improving your golf game, focus on yourself, develop your own qualities, become consistent, productive, improve your own game, the winner in golf is not the one who beats the other players, the winner is the one who beats himself, who worked on improving his own game. The winner is the one who outdid his old game the most. Period!

"You are magnificent when you accept all of who you are without judgment"

In life, winning means outdoing your old self, your old ways, your old strategy, your old views of people, and more importantly yourself. It is also important to never let external observers decide if you are doing the right things or not. Because of our ego's desire to be validated, respected, and loved... we act and do stupid things just so others think well of us, and we lose sight of the real game, and the real opponent, which is our need for our ego to be stroked. However, when we focus on just improving ourselves, becoming better than we were the day before, there is no other outcome but a winning outcome. Validation, respect and love are all verbs; they are actions that need to come from inside out, not the other way around.

When a great golfer is losing, he/she does not use the excuse that "the wind" caused me to lose, the great golfer admits, I did not develop a strategy within myself to not let the wind dictate my game. In life the wind is what others think of us. If you go outside on a windy day and try chasing it... you'll never catch it and you will find yourself exhausted trying, but if you focus on being better grounded within yourself, you won't even know the wind is there. You will have control of the outcome of your own game, and since we've already discussed that that game is focused on adding value to the pie, of creating values for others, everyone will win along with you.

Love does not look for you

Most of us have tunnel vision; it makes us prone to pigeonhole people upon first meeting them. We just see a fragment of a person and our mind often interprets what we see as a fault. Faultfinding is a habit; but focusing on the strengths of others is also a habit. See everyone you meet or think of as extending love, or as being harmless and sending out a call for help, which is a request for love. Learn to see everyone as you would an infant.

The faults we see in others, are nothing more than a call for help, it is our own system telling us that we have some transformation to make, it is our way to acknowledge ourselves for who we really are, it is like standing in front of a mirror, and the mirror talking back at us, telling us who we really are.

For example, we may feel inclined to correct or attack a rude waitress at a restaurant, if instead some voice whispered the truth in our ear – that the waitress' husband had died two days before, that she's worried about finances, or that her oldest child was recently arrested for dealing drugs – then we could see the waitress, not as rude, but as fearful and calling out for love, or calling out for sharing on our part.

With any person, we have the innate capability for unconditional love. The highest gift we might be capable of offering is to overlook his or her weakness and demonstrate total acceptance, we will discuss the role acceptance plays in living a chaos free life later in this book.

"You are magnificent when you accept all of who you are without judgment"

All of us have this ability built in; we simply need to raise our consciousness of its existence and reveal it in our lives. If a room is dark, is it because there is no light there? The circuitry is in place, the bulb is in place, what do we have to do?

Flip the light switch to reveal what is already in that room.

The same principle applies to us, the circuitry is there, the capacity is there, we are all wired for love, peace and sharing – we just have to reveal it, and how do we reveal it? We flip on the switch. How do we flip on the switch to reveal Light? Without knowing where the switch is, all can be in place, but we won't have the knowledge, or consciousness level to reveal the Light, because we won't know where to find the switch.

Why is it so difficult to transform and to reveal Light and find love, peace, and fulfillment? Because as experienced adults, we may find ourselves continually recycling old judgments, vulnerability and guilt. To break this distorted cycle, we must look upon the past as archeological garbage with no recycling value.

The past is over. We find that switch, we reveal Light in our lives when we accept this simple truth and fact. But in order to concentrate on the present, we must release (forgive) others, and ourselves from all the errors of past pain and suffering.

Imagine being the parent of a chronic schizophrenic thirty-five-year-old son and trying to apply the principle of love. How is it possible?

"You are magnificent when you accept all of who you are without judgment"

It is possible by spending as much time ridding yourself of all the past painful, guilty, fearful thoughts, and experiences you have had with your son. Releasing yourself from any guilt you have about your son's condition. How?

You can do this by imagining your built up pain, is now in a trash can attached to a yellow helium balloon, and you are letting it flow away. Pay attention to how much lighter you feel. Look past your eyes and ears, remember the five senses limit our perception of reality, they don't enhance it. Choose to see this son of yours only through the window of love. Choose to see those you hold responsible for your pain, through love.

Does this mean to live in denial? No. Actually we need to get closer to our pain and find the Light hidden within it, more on this topic later in the book, for now keep reading.

Our tendency is to feel sorry for ourselves, to feel as though we are victims; these feelings are designed to keep us from not only finding, but even bothering to look for the switch in the room (our life) that turns on the Light.

Therefore to choose to see the love in an apparently difficult situation is transformational in nature, it's taking us outside of our limited five senses, and it is helping us find the switch, turning the Light on in our lives and more importantly, shining the Light onto others.

"You are magnificent when you accept all of who you are without judgment"

Happiness isn't based on events or people, or luck. It is a natural response to use blame as a defense, absolving ourselves of responsibility. It is very difficult to forgive (remember to forgive is to take responsibility for our own selves), but when we see the bits and pieces of a fragmented world, it is only a reflection of the chaos we have in ourselves.

Peace of mind and love is an internal matter. Accordingly whenever you feel that your peace is threatened by anything or anyone, repeat in your mind, "I could see peace instead of this". It is as if you are in a movie that has a horrible ending and a nice ending and as the director of that movie (as the director of your life) you can choose the ending or outcome. It is your choice, and your choice alone.

In sickness, for example, each of us has the tendency to focus only on our own discomfort – and we complain loudly to reinforce our hopelessness. We should redirect our minds away from our bodies, away from our limited five senses and center all of our attention on serving and sharing with others. Even medical science has discovered that helping others improves one's own health.

By doing this, we cease to experience our own suffering, finding meaning in the maxim: To give is to receive.

We activate love in our lives and complete fulfillment when we realize that "we are responsible for what we choose to experience; we choose the feelings we experience, and we decide upon the goals we choose to achieve; everything that seems to happen to us, we create".

If we want love in our lives, we must love first, teach love, share love, be love, and it will in turn be experienced by us in abundance. Love is the total opposite of fear, love overcomes fear. Fear causes hate, pain, and discomfort. Love overcomes all obstacles. Love is about putting others ahead of yourself, not for the sake of compassion, morals, or dogma, but because what you emanate towards others, is what you experience.

Let me repeat that "What you emanate towards others, is what you experience". You don't do a positive action because it adds to some Karmic bank account to be withdrawn later in some way; you receive the gift immediately because what you bestow onto others will be your immediate reality, and what you receive.

Every action causes a reaction. Give, share, love and you cause similar reactions in your own life – what you wish onto others channels through you.

With every effort you make to overcome your reactive nature, with every painful change you make, incredible Light will come your way and that will manifest it's self as: happiness, fulfillment, love, wealth and all you desire.

"You are magnificent when you accept all of who you are without judgment"

Understanding how to find love in life

Society defines success as fame, fortune, and achievement as perceived through the eyes of others. We convince ourselves that we will be happy when we finally make our fortune, find the perfect spouse, graduate college, or end up at the top of our business. But most people who define success in these terms are unhappy, and sadly will likely remain this way.

Happiness comes from within. There are some principles that can serve as a map that will lead us to true inner happiness. In life's journey, our natural feelings of peace, love and joy frequently become clouded by the negative forces due to our misguided beliefs or illusions we've created along the way due to external exposures.

These negative forces we've allowed to create the illusion of our own reality easily enslave us, and our subsequent reactions to them usually cause a negative outcome (or a loss of joy). Built up stress and insecurity can be eliminated by understanding how we become slaves to our self-created thought systems, influenced by external inputs.

Truly, thoughts determine attitudes. However, most people believe they are victims of their thoughts and act on all of them. Thoughts by themselves don't cause chaos, it is the actions we take because of the thoughts that can create chaos. We create all that is around us; this simple shift in thinking can be very revealing of our own happiness because we no longer feel as victims.

We choose what to act on, and our emotions/moods are then a direct result of what thought we chose to act on. Notice, it is not the thought that causes the mood, it is the course of action we take based on the thoughts, that causes the end result of either chaos of bliss.

"You are magnificent when you accept all of who you are without judgment"

Our mind is constantly justifying why we create a feeling, and then because of our five senses we convince ourselves that they are real and we become slaves to the feelings we created. We begin to believe our lies.

Only what you think about life is overwhelming, not life itself. The simple solution? If you don't like the feelings what you are thinking about, stop thinking about them, your fears are enslaving you; take control of your thoughts instead of allowing them to control you by choosing the right course of action every time.

How is this done when the feelings are so strong? Try viewing feelings as an indicator or a compass. Negative feelings tell us it is time to dismiss negative thoughts. Positive feelings tell us we are experiencing life through our consciousness, the real you.

Each of us interprets life differently. The reasons become obvious when we understand that everyone sees through the filters of his or her own unique consciousness (thought system). But when we stop judging and start appreciating people's differences, we can learn a great deal about ourselves from them. Why? Because we are all linked, we all came from the same place, and each of us although different, is uniquely interdependent on each other. When the world not only understands this principle, but lives by it, there will be peace, and life will never cease to exist.

Any form of condemnatory judgment, hatred, or self-righteousness only contaminates the pure consciousness of the chaos free living real you. It's as if we have the Light on in a room, but we cover our eyes so we can't see it. Conversely, higher levels of understanding will come natural from positive feelings that surface when judgmental thoughts are dismissed.

"You are magnificent when you accept all of who you are without judgment"

We raise our consciousness every time we dismiss judgment of others, and more importantly judgments about ourselves.

When we are in a high mood we see things one way, when we are in a low mood we see the same things differently. For example, you are at the checkout line of your favorite food grocer, and your Light consciousness would let someone go in front of you, perhaps because he/she is in a hurry, and only has 2 items. However, if your fear of being taken advantage of takes over, you may reason with yourself, I am in a hurry too, we are all in a hurry, he/she can wait like the rest of us.

Now imagine, you walk out the store and strangely you get into some kind of accident that you might have avoided because you were in the store an extra 5 minutes. Sometimes we are given opportunities to alter the outcome of our life in a positive way, but we let our fear based thought system take over, and the actions we take as a result ruin everything. We don't often see the logic and perfection to an otherwise imperfect life.

Our negative moods are created by us by acting on negative thoughts, we build the house we live in, and we build with negative bricks. The secret is knowing that the moods are a result of the actions we took or did not take on the bad thoughts. A quiet mind allows us to choose our course of action on the thoughts coming in; our mood depends on this. Living a chaos free life requires great discipline not to let fears and judgmental thoughts run their course; meaning they can happen – but we should not act on them.

"You are magnificent when you accept all of who you are without judgment"

Having a quiet mind is listening without judgment.

Sometimes the simple realization that it is just a thought that requires no action be taken will be enough to immediately raise your level of consciousness. Sometimes the thoughts cause people to act in an out of control fashion, and the resulting moods can be devastating.

If you find yourself having raging thoughts of anger, resentment, difficulty focusing, and the actions you take on those thoughts cause chaos in your life, don't dismiss the possibility of neurotransmitters imbalance of the brain, and as such I am advocating taking properly prescribed medication or treatments by a professional.

In the past 15 years there has been an increase of 400% in Bi-Polar Disorder, mostly because unlike years ago when it was demonized, science is beginning to find treatments for imbalances that cause people to act in ways that creates chaos in their lives. These same people are geniuses, yet lead extraordinary difficult lives. People like Sir Isaac Newton, Mark Twain, Galileo, Michelangelo, Pablo Picaso, President Lincoln, and countless others were all manic depressive; they made amazing contributions to the betterment of mankind, yet I side with how difficult it must have been to live in their own minds, and within themselves, yet choose to be value creators. It takes an incredible amount of self discipline to lead an extraordinary chaos free life, if you suffer from such a disorder. Do take advantage of all that is at your disposal through modern sciences if you are one struggling with this.

Gratitude can also help in altering a bad mood too. Just by appreciating your health, talents, children or simply a beautiful object, you begin to want to emanate happiness and love, rather than fear.

"You are magnificent when you accept all of who you are without judgment"

Letting go of destructive ideas

Everything about life is about relationships, but we frequently hold false assumptions about relationships. Here are some false ideas:

Love is blind: Love is not blind. When in love, we notice differences and see them as interesting, and endearing rather than faults. We see things as we should every day. We see things without judgment. Imagine if we could do this in our relationships all the time. We would be in love all the time.

It is important to be compatible: The notion that people have to think about and enjoy doing the same things to be compatible is simply not true. It is another illusion our fears create. By respecting differences, we all have the ability to be compatible. When we remove judgment, and let go of our fears, our consciousness will find all kinds of ways to be happy in a relationship.

We will be happy when circumstances change: You cannot experience joy by focusing on circumstances and what isn't there and probably never will be. Get rid of the should, and the should nots, and start seeing what is. It's like the woman who complains about her husband snoring at night, and then wishing she could give anything to have him back when he's passed away.

Jealousy: This is my favorite; it took me 14 years to overcome this one. Jealousy is imagined fear, insecurity and possessiveness caused by unfounded assumptions or imagined ideas about how another person thinks or feels, which leads to distrust or blame. All barriers that limit clear, real, happy thinking.

"You are magnificent when you accept all of who you are without judgment"

Anything worth doing is worth doing well: Like many ideas we fabricate, this is just not so. If doing well simply meant putting your heart in it, or enjoying it, the saying would be a positive help to us. But most often we define doing a thing well as executing it perfectly – a judgment of what is ideal. Where does judgment come from? Fears. The greatest treasure – joy and happiness in doing, should replace judgment.

When happiness is more important to you than anything else, you will be happy. How is this possible? There will be no room for thoughts that can jeopardize your happiness. Understanding this changes how we see things, everything and everyone in our world looks different. It may often seem as though others have changed, but it is our thoughts (our consciousness) and thus, our reality, and thus our feelings that have changed.

When we give love, we get love not necessarily because others give it back to us, but because love will emanate through us and within us. We will channel it through us and outward to others.

Remember this basic principle: You are what thoughts you act on! You are not what you think; you are what you act on. It is only what you act on that is manifested thinking, and what you manifest is who you are.

"You are magnificent when you accept all of who you are without judgment"

In the beginning

The story in the Bible of Adam and Eve is the ultimate metaphor for how we began our journey towards activating the higher self within. Our desire to become the creators instead of the created. The path chosen was to separate from being One with the Light in order to earn back the right to be One with the Light. To become God-Man.

The Bible speaks that he would "positively die" if he ate of the fruit of knowledge of good and evil, and he did die after 900 years. He was complete and whole, and One with the Light, but desired to create the source of his fulfillment from within.

The amazing thing is that the only reason the Tree of Knowledge, the cause effect reality, the reality of judgment exists is because we keep creating it and allowing it to exist, yet we created it with a purpose.

We have forgotten that we were One consciousness, but because the feeling was so great and so fulfilling, yet lacking something, we created a reality construct to earn our fulfillment.

We were lacking the very quality that creates true and lasting fulfillment in life. The ability to emanate that which causes fulfillment.

The secret to the Light of the Tree of Life, is that it is not something you grab, it is something you generate from within, because it is already always on. But conversely the Tree of Knowledge is a reality we actually created. When we want total fulfillment, we don't have to create it, we simply have to accept it as existing.

The only thing we create, with our fears and judgments, is the realm of chaos; it's a purposeful realm, and this is what we are about to uncover.

"You are magnificent when you accept all of who you are without judgment"

Adam was completely unified with all existence, both physical and supernal. He was not only One with all around him, He was One with the Creator force. When he sought after the idea of becoming God-Man, he actually created an alternative dimension, the dimension of the Tree of Knowledge. This system mimics the system of the Tree of Life, but the energy flowing in and out of this dimension comes with a catch: Chaos.

Within this dimension we constructed a system that would challenge us back into higher unity. This challenging system manifests in the illusion of separation that is fostered by religion, nationalism, altruism, and all the things that "seem" good for mankind, but at the heart of it, they don't help mankind with the real task: that of attaching oneself to the Tree of Life reality. You can say it was a system created, and powered up by illusions to blind and challenge man's return to the Endless Fulfillment of the Light – the Tree of Life. I will go into more details on how we return to this state of existence towards the end of the book, for now keep on reading.

Since Adam, man (by man, I am referring to the human race) has been racing to fight against the reconciliation of separation from the Light, the acceptance of the only true reality, that of perfect immortality. Man's physical duality tendency to seek external authorities for fulfillment and guidance is what causes all the chaos we experience. We broke away to earn our fulfillment, yet we keep seeking for something external of ourselves to be fulfilled.

Every biblical character exemplifies that struggle and shows how some perfected one aspect of completeness, in fact several together make up the whole of what we should strive for; giants like Abraham, Isaac, Jacob, Moses, Aaron, Joseph, and David. Each of them perfected an aspect of our path back to higher unity, but it is up to our generation to finish the job.

"You are magnificent when you accept all of who you are without judgment"

When we realize that we have all we need within ourselves, meaning within the reality of our consciousness, we will ignite the power of immortality, the concept of uniting heaven and earth. The process is not easy, but what are the alternatives?

Death or an immortal perfect, totally fulfilling existence.

You see we live simultaneously in many "rooms" and at many levels.

Jesus described it as the "many mansions". We spend our lives shifting through these levels of consciousness, rarely aware of their structure. Would it help if we were aware? You Bet!

The dimensions are a readily communicable self-reference system of the highest order. They can provide an experiential, "street smart" yet philosophical set of lenses, capable of observing and ordering life in both its visible and invisible spectrums.

As individuals (and humanity as a whole) we need to accept the general principals of co-creation, and expand into our conscious evolution. New and improved self-referencing systems are being summoned into play; they are expanded-spectrum techniques (a.k.a technologies) of becoming God.

In order to understand Jesus' message one must first know the distinction between the conscious mind, and the non-conscious mind. Light consciousness vs. body consciousness. With that knowledge Jesus' message becomes clear, and so does any other story from the Bible.

"You are magnificent when you accept all of who you are without judgment"

The significance of the two ways of thinking is clearly defined. This way of thinking involves an understanding of the right hemisphere of the brain verses the left hemisphere, and the system that unifies both – the central system that is made up of our human body.

The left hemisphere (body consciousness) is our survival mechanism... automatic reactions to sights, sounds and emotions; it is based on a reactive operating system. Faced with dangerous situations one must react quickly and automatically... totally immersed in the here and now. Also for survival skills one must be able to recognize the overall picture, to grasp the larger perspective.

However our left hemisphere has a major flaw as far as Light consciousness is concerned. That is, it has no judgmental ability, no ability to reason.

Therefore man created social "codes of conduct" necessary for people to live harmoniously in a society. Moses' Ten Commandments is an example of a code of conduct to follow. Notice that all ten commands relate to objective behavior... there is no inner reason given as to why these commands are necessary, read at face value.

However there was a powerful dualism to the commandments, a Light consciousness awakening that Moses tried to help the Israelites to see, and some had that awakening but the majority did not, hence why they did not accomplish the task, which was to achieve immortality.

"You are magnificent when you accept all of who you are without judgment"

When they crossed the Red sea, one man entered the Red sea with certainty that the Red sea would split and his consciousness was so powerful, so full of certainty that it did split. In fact it is written that God asked Moses, when Moses reached out to God asking God to split the Red sea "Why are you calling me, when you have the technology to do this yourself".

The technology was the power of Light Consciousness which when fully activated unifies the right and left hemispheres using the central system (ourselves); when activated unites Heaven and Earth, in fact the formula in the Torah for activating such power within was recorded three times with 72 Hebrew letters, which were the mathematical formula that when properly added up, sort of speak, produce man's ability to accomplish anything, from splitting Red seas to living eternally without pain, without dishonesty.

Even though to us it is self evident why these commands are valid, it was not until the later prophets and especially with Jesus that the inner reasons for this behavior was known.

The body conscious man lacked introspection and could not know for himself what was moral or immoral. This explains many of the mysteries of the Old Testament when a tribe favored by God would conquer another tribe, kill the men, women and children and take all of their goods... cattle, sheep, etc.

"You are magnificent when you accept all of who you are without judgment"

There was no concept of justice, compassion, or wrong-doing on their part. When we read these stories today, we cannot reconcile that kind of behavior with God's condolence. In the light of the body consciousness mind, however, these actions become clear. There is no blame. The body consciousness man felt emotions strongly, just as we see in nature when a mother lion fiercely protects her young.

A major factor in becoming conscious and understanding Jesus' message is introspection... not just feeling emotions as all animals do and reacting automatically to those emotions, but understanding emotions. Without understanding emotions no concept of justice or compassion could emerge.

The interaction of the feeling left hemisphere (body consciousness) with the rational, objective tight hemisphere (Light consciousness) allows fully integrated Tree of Life consciousness to emerge. One chief factor is the ability to be objective, to put aside your emotions, and weigh a situation honestly... a feature body consciousness man could not do. With this ability to be objective a man can think in terms of the past and the future, not just in the present, in the here and now, as the left hemisphere does.

With that ability a man can think in terms of changing his behavior.

Jesus' emphasized forgiveness and compassion. Jesus was the cadre of transformation towards self honesty and love. The world we live in is a reflection of who we are inwardly as individuals.

As we have already discussed, forgiveness is about being responsible productive accountable people.

"You are magnificent when you accept all of who you are without judgment"

Our businesses, our schools, our governments are all run by individuals, and the laws, and traditions that we believe in or allow to exist. The formulas of the equations we give power to, determine our outer conditions.

It is only as we understand ourselves, what is good for us and what is bad for us, that we can we put forth the right actions for a good life, and this honesty integration allows us to also extend that same privilege to others.

That introspection, that getting in touch with and understanding our own emotions, leads to the conscious awareness of what is moral, good and right. That process lies at the heart of Jesus' message. Through this route a surprise emerges, Jesus' call to the weary, the suffering, and the lonely was a constant theme throughout his work.

For, those who are unhappy in some way are the most likely to introspect, for when we reach our lowest point do we awaken the desire for change, that awakening is when we activate consciousness.

Also "following his example" with the difficult trials he had to face is a way toward introspection, a major route to consciousness and the knowledge and wisdom of the "Kingdom of God".

This is why he was quoted saying, that the road to the kingdom of God is narrow and full of turmoil and tests. What did he mean by this?

"You are magnificent when you accept all of who you are without judgment"

Simply put, the process of integrating honesty into one's life only happens when one transforms the dishonest, illusionary belief system or formulas one has given power to which inevitably cause the fall, and only at that time, one has no choice but to either replace one illusion for the other (generating temporary fulfillment) or to fully integrate honesty and awaken consciousness (the God within), which is eternal.

This conscious way of thinking coincides roughly with the rule of King David in the Old Testament. Moses lived in the thirteenth century B.C. which puts Abraham, the first illuminati, even earlier. Historically, the early books of the Bible are stories of body consciousness men. Those who lived by codes of conduct handed down to them by authority figures. For example Noah listened but did not challenge, hence the great flood story is an example of a missed opportunity to awaken the consciousness of immortality.

The Old Testament prophets give a vivid picture of the awakening of consciousness in man, and the giants we read about, were harmonized beings who were not just driven by their left hemisphere (body consciousness), but by their right hemisphere (Light consciousness), and thus could create laws, standards, and provide guidance to those who for the most part lived by only their animalistic left hemisphere impulses.

There are two major stages to consciousness; to becoming aware. The first stage has to do with ethics and moral behavior. And this requires complete honesty. In following Jesus' example, he said you must die and be reborn. This is a metaphor, of course, but you must die to the old ways of thinking which keep you locked into the reality of fear, to be born into the reality of love.

"You are magnificent when you accept all of who you are without judgment"

Through introspection and examination you come to realize that contrary to church doctrines and religious beliefs you must act in your own best interest, put yourself first, have constructive desires and have a healthy concept of your own self worth. You must learn to love yourself first, in order to love your neighbor, for only when you integrate honesty within can you also see honesty outside of yourself.

Religious teachings and beliefs handed down to us say that we must be selfless, let go of desire and put others first, when in reality Jesus and other spiritual/consciousness giants were teaching to transform desire, our power, into beings complete within ourselves, for only being complete within ourselves can we then put the puzzle together, or fit into the other pieces of the puzzle who are also complete and unique within themselves.

By trying to act upon the laws of religious beliefs in our daily lives, we setup a major ethical and psychological conflict. Because all of these principles act against the nature of man.

Jesus wanted every man to develop consciousness. Putting yourself first allows you to be a whole person... a whole person who can produce and contribute to society.

Putting others first and being selfless creates an inner conflict which puts you out of control of your life... and makes you assume that other people are also at your disposal. By contrast, a man who follows his own self interest extends that same right, and respect to every other individual.

"You are magnificent when you accept all of who you are without judgment"

Unfortunately, many who intellectually advocate self interest do not inwardly understand the true nature of this important characteristic. Honest introspection would do so. This is just one example of the many religious beliefs that go against an individual's true nature, the nature of the real you.

Through introspection and having to meet reality in your daily life, you discover this fact... until one by one every false doctrine is seen through.

Then you are no longer divided against yourself but become whole... one with your true nature. Once you have achieved this understanding you are ready to achieve the second major step to consciousness.

The second major stage to consciousness is to become your own authority. This was clearly evident with Jesus who spoke with authority... and we are supposed to follow his example, which is the secret behind the words "to walk in the steps of Jesus".

In speaking with authority Jesus completely amazed the people because no religious leader of the time spoke in such a manner. Jesus and his disciples broke many of the religious laws of his time. When confronted by the Pharisees, Jesus said that laws were made for man, not man for the laws.

"You are magnificent when you accept all of who you are without judgment"

Abraham the Patriarch, came to this conclusion on his own, he in fact was the very first to become his own authority, before him the likes of Noah just listened to the body consciousness mind. He was commanded to build the ark and he did, he never challenged God, or even had the awakening that he could change the fate of all mankind. That was the first test of learning about immortality and earning our route to be becoming God-Man, a test which Noah failed.

Millenniums later, you take R. Shimon bar Yochai, (this is just a theory but, Shimon means Lightening, and Bar Yochai means Son of Thunder, which were titles given to Apostle John by Jesus). R. Shimon bar Yochai not only wrote the code for awakening consciousness known as the Zohar, but a story tells of how he challenged God himself, when the angel of death had said to him that God had decreed again that man should be destroyed, just as he did with Noah, but R. Shimon bar Yochai responded that this would not be so, because of him being righteous in the world.

He had such an awakened mind, he was so complete that he himself encompassed all of life within himself and as such had more power than the external authority known as God, over the world. In fact the story shows how we as humans create the outcome of life; we give power to everything, not the other way around. Ask yourself the question. What is more important the table which a meal sits on, or the meal it's self?

One could say the meal. But without the table, the meal could not be presented; the meal could not be, for the meal needs to be presented by the table. In the ten dimensions of the Tree of Life, the table is called Malchut. Earth and physical existence exists within Malchut. Without Malchut, the Light would have no place to enter, without the Light Malchut would be dark and empty. One needs the other and one powers up the other. The table or Malchut is very important. That's you and me!

Everything, from angels to demons to God is powered up by us, by our consciousness, by the value we give to the equations, to the mathematical formulas of our consciousness.

Once a person is conscious of ethical and honest behavior, and the inner and psychological reasons why that behavior is essential to his and others' happiness, then he is ready to become his own authority.

Being your own authority has rules, you must know where you fit within the dimensions and how to properly create such authority, for without the flow of the Light you cannot exist, and without proper awe for the Light you cannot receive such authority. Authority is not about power; it is about being full of Light and accepting the role of being a channel of Light.

However, a person must start living a self directed and self interested life to build the confidence needed to break through to the second stage... to become his own authority.

That's why Jesus spoke in metaphors and parables to the crowds. You cannot make a huge leap in consciousness until the groundwork is first laid.

Developing consciousness and becoming your own authority is clearly Jesus' message. And in order to be your own authority you must break with all authorities, including the mystical authority "God" as religion teaches it to be.

All mystical literature states this... that you must give up even the spiritual. And all mystics came to this stage, but they would not tell you what they discovered. I wrote this book so as to make you aware of this, purely out of self interest for returning to a state of bliss along with you. Together we can and we will live a chaos free life.

"You are magnificent when you accept all of who you are without judgment"

The few who did speak of such wisdom were ostracized or even killed. Today is different; today you are reading this, because the world is truly ready, the secrets no longer need to be among a select few.

Realizing that all mystical experiences come from your own right hemisphere and not from outside of yourself or from "God", comes as a great shock.

The realization produces tremendous anger... anger at those who know the truth but write books encouraging you to follow the misleading beliefs. In the final analysis, you know that you are responsible for your own involvement... for your own gullibility.

Once knowing the truth one recognizes that the insights one has had are no different from the insights that scientists, businessmen and other creative people have.

It's just the interpretation that was wrong... they were not mystical insights coming from outside yourself... coming from "God"; they were insights that came as a result of expanded consciousness.

That's the final identification all mystics make.

God does not exist as its own entity, God is expressed through you and me and it is expressed through love. It's a frequency, a signal, a wave, and we are all part of it, we are not separate from God, We just need to remember why we started on this journey in the first place, to remember who we truly are. We discover God through love and with this realization one can begin to reach full consciousness, and can begin to live a chaos free life.

"You are magnificent when you accept all of who you are without judgment"

Fully conscious people can step into what Jesus called "The Kingdom of God"

This is the key secret of why self transformation is so important, because universal consciousness cannot happen without the added value of each member contributing his and her own essence to the collective.

The collective, as already discussed, is God and we experience God when we collectively emanate love towards one another. This does not require that we all walk the same path.

A path is what it is, a path – it is not the end destination. Our purpose is to reach the end destination "The Kingdom of God", how each of us get's there, is within our free will to decide, but getting there is the only truly noble and worthy cause to center our lives around.

We are like puzzle pieces, if all the puzzle pieces of a puzzle were the same shape and form, you could never complete the puzzle, hence we must see ourselves as the only unique piece of the puzzle, but that without ourselves, and without our neighbor we cannot complete the picture.

Our single goal in life is, and should be completing this picture, returning to the state of Oneness, through the earning process we've put in motion since Adam.

It does not matter what your religious or spiritual beliefs are, because we are ultimately on the same journey, and we will end up at the intended destination, no matter what... it is our destiny to enter the "Kingdom of God".

The entry way is not as far as it may seem, it is right there, within you.

"You are magnificent when you accept all of who you are without judgment"

The secret of activating "The Kingdom of God" within

Jesus spoke of a "Sacred Secret", so did all the Apostles.

The Sacred Secret is simple, and it was of great significance 2000 years ago, as it is today.

Up to the time of Jesus and his contemporary, the relationship man had with God was for the most part that of a Lord/Servant relationship, upon the revelation of that time the secret revealed was that all humans, all creations are a spark of God, peers to the concept of God, not under God but actually the contrary. Remember the idea of the meal being served on the table, the table is important. We are the table.

Humans are a resonance of this powerful energy called God, the actions we take in life based on honesty create fulfillment, the actions based on dishonesty, create chaos.

When Jesus spoke of himself as the son of God, he was referring to the fact that we are all God within and only in realizing that we have the power of God, meaning we all have the power to be our individual Messiah, can we actually bring the energy or consciousness of the Messiah. He was killed for claiming to be a spark of the Creator, which we all are.

Of course many interpreted that Jesus himself was God, because the concept of accepting oneself as God, a spark of God was blasphemy to many at that time, but because he could do miracles, which we are all capable of doing if we actually activate that power within us, many created a new dishonesty around him.

"You are magnificent when you accept all of who you are without judgment"

Publishing insights such as this, would have surely resulted in death back then, as many will call what you are reading, as written from the Anti-Christ, but many who are striving to integrate honesty based consciousness, will see it for what it is, a breath of fresh air.

Even when Moses was about to reveal the secret to immortality, the power of fully integrated honesty based consciousness, the people who had been slaves for so long, who remained controlled by the body consciousness mind, could not possibly understand their own power to bring immortality, or the Messiah consciousness.

Even after they had crossed the Red Sea and tasted their own powers, they still simply could not connect to the concept of having that spark within them, they stayed in their body consciousness state of mind. Followers instead of leaders, effect instead of cause, created instead of creators.

The entire story of Exodus is the struggle of man to leave behind the body consciousness mind, the need to give external things power (idols, mysticism, even the concept of God as many interpret God to be a separate entity of ourselves), and activate the conscious immortal mind.

Leaving Egypt was a code for leaving the enslavement of the body consciousness mindset, and the promise land was the end goal of reaching the consciousness of immortality, the time they spent in the dessert is a code for the step by step integration of consciousness, the leaving behind of dishonest authorities, the power we give to external things, and the realization that there is only consciousness, and only in fully integrating this honesty can one reach immortality.

The story is not about something that took place thousands of years ago; the story is about us, you and me, today. The story is our story.

"You are magnificent when you accept all of who you are without judgment"

The dessert is a place where your only mode of survival is to tap into your creative mind, your consciousness which will guide you out of any situation. This consciousness is the very connection to the Creator that gives us the power to become whole, to become complete; only in achieving this connection can we say that we have become our own authority – meaning our connection with the Creator, returns us to a state of completeness just as Adam was.

All religious people are still in Egypt and only a few who leave, who go through the dessert, the process for awakening the consciousness, actually reach the promise land, or at least the entry way to it.

Religious people seeking SOMEONE to save them, waiting for the Messiah and don't realize it is within all of us, we are all the Messiah, if we learn to free ourselves for Egypt (the body consciousness mind) and cross the dessert (the process of self integration of honesty) and reach the promise land (fully integrated honest consciousness) of immortality.

The Sacred Secret is that we are all collectively the God consciousness, and we have a duty to activate our own spark of this formula, for the formula to actually produce the result intended, a chaos free reality.

Think of yourself as the math equation, and formula that is missing from the answer to the ultimate math test, the test that will produce eternal fulfilling life from the correct answer.

At the era of John the Baptizer and Jesus, there was an attempt to change all that, which sent the manipulators of man, the consciousness cheaters, in an uproar.

"You are magnificent when you accept all of who you are without judgment"

Every quote of those Apostles in the New Testament speak of the Sacred Secret, that being: The power of the God within us, the ability and the duty of each of us to bring immortality, but the ego of the ruling class did not want people to know this Sacred Secret, for there would be no religion today if those Apostles had succeeded in their work.

The Sacred Secret is becoming known to more and more people today, the consciousness of slavery/victim (body consciousness mind) is diminishing.

Every stream of spirituality is printing books on immortality, on consciousness, on the life and story of Jesus. Why? Because there is a collective awakening happening, just as the illuminati of old and new, predicted.

The "Sacred Secret" is that we are sparks of God, and sons of God, and that we collectively are God, only when we change waiting for the Messiah, and realize that the Messiah is within all of us, that being the Sacred Secret, will we actually benefit from the promise of the Messiah consciousness, which has only one answer and result from the equation:

TOTAL CHAOS FREE FULFILLMENT.

"You are magnificent when you accept all of who you are without judgment"

The secret behind Jesus' our Lord's Prayer

Our Lord's Prayer as adopted by the Church of England 1977

Our Father in Heaven,
Hallowed be your Name,
Your kingdom come, Your will be done,
On earth as in Heaven.
Give us today our daily bread.
Forgive us our sins, As we forgive those
Who sin against us.
Lead us not into temptation
But deliver us from evil.
For the kingdom, the power, And the glory are yours
Now and forever.
Amen.

Our Lord's prayer in the original Aramaic

אבון דבשמיא

נתקדש שמך

תאתא מלכותך

נהוא צביני

איכנא דבשמיא אף בארעא

הב לן לחמא דסונקנן יומנא

ושבוק לן חובין איכנא דאף חנן שבקן לחייבין

ולא תעלן לנסיונא

אלא פצן מן בישא

Our Lord's Prayer consciousness translation

Consciousness, may you be the Light within us -- may you be made useful
May you unite our mind and thinking
May all results in our lives be of the desire of our consciousness within,
As in desire, so in all physical forms and actions.
May we produce value each day and expanded consciousness
May we break loose of the cords of illusions of our body consciousness mind, as we release the strands of dishonesty.
Don't let external powers delude us,
but free us from what is external of ourselves and holds us back.
From consciousness is born all ruling will,
The power and the life to do,
The song that beautifies all,
From age to age it renews.
I affirm this with my whole complete spirit and body.

"You are magnificent when you accept all of who you are without judgment"

The sacred secret

The sacred secret is - that we must activate the consciousness of God within ourselves, actually that we must let go of our need to be ruled by external forces, even what we call God; meaning an external power that is separate from us. When we accept God as connected to us, and when we accept that we are not separated from our Creator, then we will have reached the full consciousness of the Messiah.

Jesus gave his life to prove this, he died a free man. He died with the desire to prove that it is best to become the Messiah, immortal and free, than to live a life of dishonesty full of external controls, a life of a slave.

When the majority of humans live by this consciousness, the collective power will bring total immortal fulfillment. The promise of eternal life in the Kingdom of God, Jesus spoke of, will be realized, for the Kingdom of God is none other than eternal life we as humans will create by integrating honesty, and expanded God consciousness; by reuniting with the Creator force in all of us, as One.

Think of yourself as a television station transmitter, and receiver all at the same time, what you do (the programming you decide to upload to the satellite, or what we call the power of the Universe, God, whatever you want to call it) determines what programming you also receive.

"You are magnificent when you accept all of who you are without judgment"

Junk out, junk in, good out, good in. If you do positive actions, you send positive programming to the satellite, the satellite beams that programming back down to you and also to others and since you tuned into positive programming (because of your actions), you end up being surrounded by others who also do the same.

When you send negative programming to the satellite, you can't expect to receive positive programming, let alone be surrounded by those who are also tuned into positive programming.

What you do comes back to you with all that surrounds you. Negative actions, draw down negative reactions; positive actions draw down positive reactions. The satellite does not judge, the satellite simply executes your command.

The satellite is the concept of the Divine energy of God, it broadcasts the programming we create, good or bad – hence there is no one to blame, or to thank for the results in your life, but you.

What you create will beam back down to you. Nimrod used this power to try to dominate the world; he knew the secret to activating the signal: UNITY.

When positive actions are done by you, me, and many others, we create unity; unity is the multiplier that causes more positive results to manifest.

God – The satellite broadcast station of the Universe

Society's personification of God, the concept of the frequency of God being separate from us, is a road back out of higher unity. This is the "God is great– I am not worthy" syndrome. Religion, as it is currently practiced on our planet, traditionally presupposes a separation from divinity as its establishing postulate, yet we have also discussed that we created such as a force of opposition so we could earn our unity back.

This is an unfortunate body consciousness dimensional organizing principal, which literally guarantees the sincere adherent, devotee, or follower of a religious thought lack of access to their own organic permanent state of well being through Light consciousness within them.

The body consciousness mind succeeded in quarantining Earth from the affairs of universal society, by creating a separate figure that became known as God. This could be a happy or angry God, a living or dead savior figure or guru, or entire panoplies of gods, goddesses, or Buddha. The road to religious hell, as they say, is paved with good intentions.

Well meaning and intentioned, it stirs the dimensional soup. However, its very existence also, like religion, implies an absence of the desired end. Therefore, its potency is limited. But it has served, and does serve a purpose on the journey started by us through Adam.

For example when people pray: "Oh God, please make me stronger, wiser, etc" it is actually a very powerful expression of the lack of these desired qualities in a person. We are - in the world of thought as well as the physical body – a reflection of what we digest. Remember the metaphor of the television station and the satellite?

"You are magnificent when you accept all of who you are without judgment"

Garbage in, Garbage out. Duality in, Duality out. God in, God out. I am in, I am out. Therefore a glass ceiling of sorts is placed around prayer, with possible outcomes, and eventualities limited to the belief system of the person praying.

Prayers emitting from a person in the electromagnetic grid dimensions will get an outcome reflecting the permanence of duality. Once one is focused outside of themselves in the physical world of cause and effect, they become an unwitting pawn of the closed loop system of that reality.

That is, until they cross the bridge. Then the pawn, reprogrammed, can be turned into a Queen or King. The intentional crossing of the unity within, and our surrendered shifting or rising of self, activates our "connection" or aspect of our higher self.

Notice I did say self, as in individuality for only when we work on becoming who we are meant to be, can we share those gifts with the rest of the collective.

This is the key secret of why self transformation is so important, because universal consciousness cannot happen without the added value of each member contributing his and her own essence to the collective.

As discussed, if all the puzzle pieces of a puzzle were the same shape and form, you could never complete the puzzle, hence when we see ourselves as the only unique piece of the puzzle, but that without ourselves and without our neighbor we cannot complete the picture, we raise the value of all existence in the process.

"You are magnificent when you accept all of who you are without judgment"

The signal is a bit fuzzy – check your dial and tune back in

Religious teachings are very seductive.

They hold out the promise of wisdom. This is especially enticing to someone who has problems in life. You think you are going to gain something extremely important.

Religious teachings are filled with spiritual mysteries that need solving, and solving mysteries is something everyone likes to do. Indeed, mystery is a real drawing power of all forms of religion.

People who go into the spiritual path on a deep level do so because they are seeking honesty, enlightenment, fairness. They desire a world where honesty prevails, where fairness and compassion are the rulers. They're seeking an ideal way to live, and deal with others.

What the dedicated student of religion eventually discovers is the core of religion is in reality non-existent.

Those few dedicated students who reach this breakthrough either leave in disgust (a minority) or are made "masters" and "teachers" and continue to perpetuate the teachings.

They rationalize... "the people", "the masses" need to believe in a higher power, and need the guidance, and morality provided by the religious doctrines. They think "people need structure", and this is true, but only as a "step" towards self realization.

They play a role in the opposition on our journey we started with Adam, and as such they are playing a role in the process we all agreed was needed to get to the end destination.

"You are magnificent when you accept all of who you are without judgment"

After being a dedicated pupil and active lecturer of religious teachings for over two decades, I was astonished when I finally broke through to enlightenment – realizing there was no higher power looking out after our lives that is "separate" from ourselves.

Even more astonishing is when religious students realize most of their leaders have also broken through to this same level. They know there is no higher separate power outside of yourself, other than the real you waiting to be activated.

Those students who struggle for years and finally break through are then made the masters and teachers themselves.

According to religious and mystical leaders, belief is good for the common people who need their belief in God, and belief is based on guidance from a higher authority. But this is what we decided to create within, this is the opposite of the journey we started on with Adam.

The religious teachings take one on a psychological path which involves learning a tremendous amount about human nature.

You are strongly drawn into it, often by reading books by others who felt they had a personal relationship with God. You read and study religious literature which affirms there is a persona called God.

So you become a very strong believer. Some people may be deeply religious, and others may not be very religious at all, however if they go into the literature and study it, then they become strongly religious. It is inevitable, because what is sold is that someone other than you, will fix all your problems. Remember, this is not what we wanted, yet it is so alluring, and this is the opposition we created to overcome. Ironic, that religion teaches that Satan is in opposition to religion, when it his greatest arsenal.

Satan is also a code, it represents a force of opposition, but the true nature of this force is to help us overcome our tendency to be served, it is there to help us become God-Man.

Religion appeals to the masses because it sells you a God who will help you. That's the hook behind religious teachings -- that there's a persona called God who's going to help you, someone outside of your own sphere of existence who is a higher power than you.

It's the essence of what attracts most people to religion. They're looking for someone or something to help them. In addition, most people want to believe in God and in heaven, because taking responsibility for oneself is way too real, and difficult.

The religious or mystic path is a process one goes through which can be compared to a scientific experiment. The scientist takes a theory and through objective experiment proves the theory to be true or false.

The student of religion takes a religious doctrine, puts it into practice in his life, and proves to himself if the doctrine is true or false. The student's life is the experiment.

What the religious student discovers is religious doctrines put one in a double bind; something impossible to achieve.

There are three major doctrines.

One doctrine is to give up personal desire, which leads to a state of no motivation. Through experience, you learn this doctrine, if fully implemented, would literally result in death. Thus, it is impossible to achieve and is, therefore, in reality, anti-life.

"You are magnificent when you accept all of who you are without judgment"

The second doctrine impossible to achieve is to be selfless, and at the same time develop spiritual character.

The third doctrine which also acts against your nature is to do the will of God... to have an authority figure over you. Over the years, as you live through real-life experiences and the experience of honestly, wholeheartedly trying to live by those three doctrines, you learn how ineffective they are.

Each new insight is a shock to your intelligence. You cannot achieve what the religious literature tells you to achieve, and be true to your own nature. It takes a long time to break through and realize this.

By acting selfless your emotions begin to rebel. Eventually your emotions rebel against someone else (God) making important decisions for you. Your nature is to grow, and develop in order to become your own authority. And the state of having no desire is worse than death.

Your emotions eventually rebel against all three of those doctrines. Through personal experience, each doctrine proves to be destructive to your own nature, and psychological health; but prove effective in awakening the real you, and therefore serve as a valuable force of opposition.

What religious students call illumination (insights from God) are actually creative insights comparable to those of any creative person... whether he is a scientist, a businessman, or an artist.

The scientist and the businessman know such insights are coming from within their own minds. The religious student thinks his insights are coming from a God. The creative process involves several stages. We can recognize the process at work in a scientist's experiment.

"You are magnificent when you accept all of who you are without judgment"

This is the same process a religious student experiences by putting into practice a religious doctrine in his or her life. By comparison below, two important concepts emerge.

1. The creative insights of the religious student or mystic come from his own mind and not from God, later in this book we'll discuss in greater details where thoughts actually come from and the role the concept of God has in our lives.

2. The religious doctrine is tested in reality to prove if it is scientifically valid. Immersing oneself into the religious doctrines, and one-by-one testing each doctrine in reality, is the process one goes through to eventually break through the hoax and become a "master:"

The Scientist	**The Mystic Path**
1. *First Insight* A theory the scientist has.	1. *First Insight* Accept a Doctrine on faith and act selfless in a contained area.
2. *Saturation* Learn everything you can about your subject.	2. *Saturation* Act selfless in the contained area until it becomes second nature.
3. *Incubation* A period in which your mind integrates all knowledge received ...including the consistent with the non-consistent.	3. *Incubation* A period in which your mind integrates your actions with your true nature.

"You are magnificent when you accept all of who you are without judgment"

<table>
<tr>
<td>

4. *Illumination*
   The creative insight. The problem is solved. A certainty that the solution is correct. A great feeling of joy.

</td>
<td>

4. *Illumination*
   The creative insight -- selfless behavior is destructive to man's nature. It is humiliating and fosters low self esteem. Selfishness creates moral characteristics. A great relief and feeling of joy.

</td>
</tr>
<tr>
<td>

5. *Verification*
   Verify your creative insight through experiments...then duplicate your experiment and verify again.

</td>
<td>

5. *Verification*
   Reject selfless behavior. Become selfish in your actions and verify the beneficial results with both yourself and with others.

</td>
</tr>
</table>

The above shows how religious students break through on the other side of religiousity. But most people who believe in God do not go into religion in such depth.

They live on the fringes of religion, and don't seriously apply the two major concepts that would eventually cause them to break through... the concept of giving up personal desire, and the concept of being selfless.

Instead they hold onto the concept of God. When you seriously immerse yourself in religion, your thoughts become so caught up in the religious ideal that you negate your true emotional response.

But at some point your insightful right-brain hemisphere is going to get through to your irrational left-brain hemisphere. And when it does, you will have broken through the flaw of giving yourself over to some external power outside of yourself.

Consider how Zen Buddhism works. The way to break through to full consciousness for Zen followers is through a process of intellectual statements called Koans.

The Koans also present the students with a double bind. For example, the Koan "One hand clapping" is to be meditated on and understood by the pupil. It makes no sense, of course, but the student tries to understand the mystery.

The purpose is to confuse, and to shock one out of their preconceived ideas... ideas that go against reality. If you have enough intensity you'll eventually break through, and realize what they're telling you to achieve goes totally against your own nature. But the real problem is practically no one achieves it.

Look how religion is spread throughout the whole world. Nearly everyone goes into it but it's just a very, very few who go into it in such depth that they see the flaw of giving yourself over to some external power outside of you.

In religion, Zen Buddhism, even the occult, an interested person goes into it like a dedicated student. One keeps studying, applying his lessons to life, and keeps advancing to the next level. After many years a handful of them make it all the way, i.e., break through to the final level.

"You are magnificent when you accept all of who you are without judgment"

That final level is realizing the flaw of giving yourself over to some external power outside of yourself, there is no power above you – you are your own authority. You see, that is the final "master" level the leaders keep telling their students to strive for – the realization that you are your own authority and that you should not, cannot seek guidance from persons, and authorities outside yourself.

Well, I was never so angry in my whole life as when I finally broke through, and realized the whole thing about a kind, benevolent God looking out for you is a hoax. Eventually I pushed aside the anger because in the final analysis, I was the one responsible for accepting the ideas in the first place, and it did serve a great purpose for me.

My anger was because everyone who goes into religion or any form of mysticism reads books, and studies the teachings of the religious/mystical leaders. Those leaders, and authors break through and realize the hoax yet they don't come back and reveal it in their works. They keep their books, and teachings on the market which entice others into this endless cycle of a world full of people who live a chaos filled life.

Everyone goes into religion in a sincere and honest way. They're seeking solutions to important problems in their lives. Yet they're enticed to go into a way of living which acts against their nature, and against the journey which started in the beginning with Adam.

And so few finally break through to realize it's all a hoax. Why is it a hoax? Because many people spend their whole life caught up living in a way they shouldn't be living, acting and doing things which go against themselves, their self interests, and they are so unhappy, resulting in more chaos in the world.

"You are magnificent when you accept all of who you are without judgment"

Why would these masters not share the truth? They're receiving a lot of adulation, and are making a living off of their teachings, ministries, and books. They have a vested interest in keeping the hoax alive.

Most religious leaders, Zen masters, and occult teachers, don't believe in an external higher power known as God. You know what they do? They rationalize. They say the masses need the concept of a higher external authority to keep them moral, or there will be more chaos, but history shows the opposite has happened to mankind, the hoax has created nothing but chaos.

They say the masses psychologically need the idea of an external God. But the general population is made up of businessmen, doctors, lawyers, architects, teachers, blue-collar workers. They're not ignorant or uneducated. The general population is smart, and self-sufficient.

The leaders keep the deception alive so they can be looked up to as highly spiritual, as masters, as making an admirable and highly respectable livelihood. The ego is involved, and most of them are blind to it as well.

It is extremely difficult to make the breakthrough, especially since the teachings also warn you of "doom" should you question the teachings, or go against them. It's a catch 22 for most people.

But those "leaders and teachers", when they break through, will never tell their followers what they learned. Instead, they use hidden terminology. They'll call someone who has broken through a Master... one who has learned wisdom. They don't tell you the wisdom he's learned is that an individual is his own authority in life, and that God is an internal energy not some external persona.

They can't tell you because then their whole profession would crumble. But they also can't tell you because this is the process we all agreed to undertake in our journey towards unity with the Light. When the time is right, everyone will know the truth... hopefully a book like this one will contribute to creating the frequency for such truths to finally be revealed.

So how can you know when a religious/mystical leader has broken through and knows the hoax? There are stages of learning a person goes through. You can recognize the stage a person is in. One who has broken through to the final stage of "enlightenment" speaks with authority and self-confidence; they also speak more in terms of technology and science, and less in terms of God.

Also they do not emphasize earlier stages of learning which they have already broken through.

The promises held out in the religious and mystical teachings all disappear when the hoax is realized. If you refuse to reveal the hoax, you can go on with your religious ministry.

Realize, however, many ministers are just as in the dark regarding the hoax as are their congregations. They, too, have not advanced to the master level. When reading a religious book you can tell by the way the author expresses himself/herself if they've broken through, i.e., they realize the hoax but they're still promoting it. You see, there are different stages the mystics discuss in their books.

As an example, there is St. Theresa of Avila who wrote a number of books.

She broke through to the full realization. She totally stopped reading religious literature. Her whole adult life was spent constantly reading and writing about the Lord. Suddenly, she completely stopped.

Why? Because she realized her visions, her trances, everything was coming from her inner self.

She didn't tell her confessor what she had realized. The priest, who had always heard her confessions, just could not get over why all of a sudden she stopped all religious reading... for that had been her passion in life. That's one of the clues – she stopped all religious reading. I know how she felt.

When I read about her life I immediately knew what had happened. She didn't tell anyone what she had learned. In her time during the Spanish Inquisition, had she revealed what she learned, she would have been burned at the stake.

Once a person breaks through the hoax to realize there is no higher external authority looking out for you, you miss the relationship you thought you had with God. The thought that reality is all there is can seem cold. It takes away the mystery, and love that communication with God provided.

Reality seems very cold at first. Yet, so liberating as you truly learn to be accountable to yourself and everyone around you and your love for others becomes genuine, not based on altruistic ideas which we'll discuss later in the book.

You can break down the religious path into four major stages. The first stage is when you're first brought in; when you first start thinking you have communication with God.

Of course, that's very joyous. Because if you believe in an external God and you believe he's chosen to communicate with you, can you imagine how that makes you feel? You experience a tremendous feeling of joy, devotion, and appreciation for being so gifted, and loved by God.

"You are magnificent when you accept all of who you are without judgment"

It also gives you a lot of courage to think that what you're doing is right. In this first stage you are enamored with the idea of signs, and miracles as taught in the Bible. But the euphoria soon passes.

The system teaches you to be irresponsible, because as long as someone outside of you is creating miracles or chaos... you never have to actually look within yourself to make the changes within to improve your own life, and this causes a problem for everyone's life.

Your own chaos, contributes to the chaos of others. The more one takes responsibility and holds oneself fully accountable, the more you can change one by one the negative traits that clearly are not producing good results in your own life or any one's life for that matter. Conversely the good you experience, is what you can share with others too.

Evelyn Underhill in her book "Mysticism" also envisioned four stages. I would like to use her grouping because they are so descriptive of what takes place.

Her descriptions affirm the religious and mystical experience.

Stage one: Awakening of the self:

Preceded by a period of discontent.

Usually a single and abrupt experience of conversion.

It's usually sudden, intense, and joyous.

(Note: One quickly learns that seeking miracles is not what the religious path is all about.)

Stage two: Purification of the self:

Purgation of imperfection in your character.

Self-simplification and self-knowledge

Contemplation

Detachment and analysis

(Note: This stage involves following the will of God, self-sacrifice in a contained area, and giving up personal desires. This is the hardest stage to go through.)

"You are magnificent when you accept all of who you are without judgment"

Stage Three: Illumination of the self:

Awakening to consciousness of reality.

Insights and a certainty about life.

Has detached himself from his chief entanglements.

Has re-oriented his life with a new and solid certitude.

Sets new standards of conduct and thought.

Introspection and turning inward deliberately to discern reality.

Has not yet reached the goal.

(Note: This stage reflects that the ideas of self-sacrifice and giving up all personal desires have been rejected because of their harmful nature to character development.)

Stage Four: Unitive life. Union:

The goal reached. A profound change in personality.

The mystics describe it as "The Spiritual Marriage".

(Note: At this stage you become your own authority and master. You recognize there is no God external of yourself and the communication you thought you had came from your own subconscious. You are no longer "divided" but are "at-one-with yourself".)

"You are magnificent when you accept all of who you are without judgment"

The first stage is obvious... the decision to devote oneself to religion, and claim its promises and "wisdom". The second stage is the longest and most difficult. It is a psychological process that involves much self examination.

The second stage is one of meditation and contemplation. I know a lot of people say meditation is a form of making your mind blank, and not thinking about anything. That's totally opposite of what actually takes place.

You are supposed to relax. If there's something bothering or upsetting you, you push that aside. Emotions will color your thinking so you can't think clearly. The idea of meditation is to get calm and push away any emotional worries. Then you start thinking about things that perfect character.

You start examining your life and your attitudes.

As you read a lot of religious literature and examine the lessons they teach, the idea they teach is to perfect your character, which means being honest, fair and compassionate.

Take sympathy and compassion. The religious idea of service to others has been so instilled throughout everyone's life. Yet, you begin to recognize how altruism can sometimes do more harm to people than good. We see an example in government handouts that have crippled generations of inner-city residents.

You realize you can feel sympathy for people but true compassion takes into account not crippling them while trying to help them. There are two major emphases in this second stage... to give up desire and to follow the will of God. But you come to realize over time no one really knows what the will of God is.

Some say the will of God means that anything in your life is there because God allows it to be there. However, you come to points where something you want to do with your life appears to be blocked. That naturally happens through living life.

But you interpret each block as the need to give up some personal desire, because God is blocking you until you sacrifice something.

The seriously religious person is brought to a stage where eventually he or she just gives up all personal interests. That stage is the worse stage to go through. You have no motivation, no interests.

I don't think anyone could go through it for very long. They would end up sick, physically and/or mentally. I know, I went through it.

In the end, one cannot live in such a state. Emotions are the fuel of our lives. If you have no desire, you have no motivation. Without desire there's no fuel or motivation to do anything. All of a sudden the heaviness in my arms went away after I got interested in something particular.

So that was a major breakthrough in my understanding and rejection of "giving up desire".

Rapidly following that insight came another major breakthrough. I was at a stage where one becomes very in-control of one's emotions. You're so guarded in your reactions, and how you act with others.

In an unguarded moment I had a major breakthrough concerning sacrifice. Whenever you stifle your true nature, like justified anger or any other natural emotion, you do not negate the emotion.

What had been happening in following the idea of sacrifice and humility was I had been stifling my emotions. They were going inward and being suppressed. In an unguarded moment those emotions had surfaced all at once and I broke down.

I realized little old ladies who go to church and practice self-sacrifice all their lives are suppressing the same emotions of anger at being manipulated, and taken advantage of by others. They too are capable of violence and rage in unguarded moments. Drive next to one, and you'll know what I mean.

Religious teachings tell you to push aside your natural emotional reactions of anger, and humiliation, and show love, and compassion instead. In reality, if something unfair or unjust happens to you then you need to address the anger or frustration.

If you don't, you suppress it. And the suppression eventually harms your self-esteem. So with me, a flood of negative emotions suddenly overcame me. I realized practicing sacrifice, and being selfless, the two concepts religion says are central to perfecting character, are wrong. Instead of building honest, genuine character, those actions result in the opposite.

"You are magnificent when you accept all of who you are without judgment"

I knew I was as spiritual as anyone else who went into religion as deeply and sincerely as I did. Yet if I could be filled with those violent emotions because of following the religious doctrines of sacrifice, and selflessness then something was terribly wrong.

It's following the doctrine of selflessness and sacrifice which caused those emotions of rage within me. Those two concepts go against man's nature.

So this realization was my first major breakthrough... coupled with the realization and rejection of giving up personal desire. Those two insights end the second stage of the mystic path. The religious student then enters the third stage with self-confidence, and a new evaluation of reality.

The concepts of selfish versus selflessness are so basic to man's character, and to his happiness that I want to elaborate on each.

Many say selfishness is cold and leaves no room for compassion. I prefer to use the term self-interest because it does away with the negative connotation of a spoiled child. However, selfishness in its true sense is the correct terminology, and definition.

The best way to grasp the differences between those two concepts is to demonstrate the character development, and the behavior which results from each concept.

The contrast of selfish versus selflessness can be demonstrated in the hero concept versus the coward concept. Everyone admires the hero. His characteristics are: strength of character, principled behavior, honesty, self-confidence, a healthy self-esteem, bravery and daring, self-respect, stands up for him/her self against great odds, is compassionate, and fair in his dealings with others.

"You are magnificent when you accept all of who you are without judgment"

Everyone despises a coward. "Wait a minute", you say, to be selfless is the same as being a coward? Since religion holds up selflessness as an ideal, people fool themselves as to what self-sacrifice really means. Because we have been so instilled by religion that selflessness is moral, we fail to recognize the consequences of such behavior.

The behavior of the selfless person is the behavior of the coward. The selfless person puts others first and self second. He fails to stand up for himself. That action causes resentment and anger toward other people to build up. In addition, he thinks others can be sacrificed as he sacrifices himself.

The selfish person's behavior is identical with the hero concept. The selfless person's behavior is identical with the coward concept.

<u>Selfish</u>	<u>Selfless</u>
1. The Hero Concept Everyone admires	1. The Coward Concept Everyone despises
2. Puts self first Result: Respects self, therefore, respects others	2. Puts self second Result: Taken advantage of, therefore, feels resentment toward others
3. In control and works hard to accomplish goals	3. Must manipulate others to achieve his goals

"You are magnificent when you accept all of who you are without judgment"

4. A strong personality	4. A weak personality
5. Self-confidence and self-esteem	5. Lack of self-confidence and low self-esteem
6. Honest and forthright	6. Hides emotional reactions, therefore, not honest with others
7. Feels secure in himself and has no desire to control others	7. Feels insecure and desires to control others in order to fill his inner void.
8. Recognizes the individual as the highest value	8. Views the individual as someone who can be sacrificed.
9. Compassionate towards others because he feels a love and respect for himself	9. Cannot feel compassion toward others because he hates himself for his cowardly actions. He disguises this self-hatred by projecting it onto others.

"You are magnificent when you accept all of who you are without judgment"

When working in accordance with his biological, emotional, and intellectual nature, man is a beautifully integrated whole. He is at one with himself. When man acts against himself in one of these areas he is at odds with himself, and the consequences can be disastrous.

An extreme example of how destructive selfless behavior can be, and how it can affect everyone in their daily lives is given below:

A few years ago a young boy about thirteen years old killed a neighboring child.

No one knew why he had killed the little fellow. Not the psychologist who interviewed him, not the counselors, not his teachers, not his parents.

But it was self evident. The TV program on this tragic incident stated the thirteen year old had been subject to insults, and humiliations all his life from his school peers. He looked a little odd. He had offset eyes. About two weeks before the murder, the thirteen-year-old asked his stepfather what to do with anger. He was told to get it out in some kind of physical exercise, like a punching bag.

The boy bruised both hands in striking the tree in front of his house, but that action didn't really address the cause of his anger. He had a justified anger because of the insults, and humiliations he had endured. But strong anger by itself does not create a murderer.

His anger turned into violence because of the self-hatred he felt... the self hatred caused by not standing up for himself... not holding himself up as a worthy individual.

"You are magnificent when you accept all of who you are without judgment"

In other words, he viewed himself as a coward and he hated the image. Violent criminals are known for their lack of remorse toward their victims. They cannot feel remorse because they feel no remorse for themselves... they feel self-hatred, and project that feeling onto their victims.

By comparison, take a person who is selfish. He stands up for himself, so no inner resentment builds up.

He feels self-respect, and extends the same self-respect to others. He has no desire to manipulate others but has the courage to be straightforward, and honest in his dealings with others.

Because he likes himself, he is capable of liking others and feeling compassion toward them. In contrast, the selfless person lacks self-confidence and has a low self-esteem; because he lets others take advantage of him.

Because he does not stand up for himself, he hides his emotional reactions, and therefore is not honest with others. He manipulates others through kindness or "feel sorry for me attitudes".

Although outwardly he professes compassion, inwardly he is filled with resentment, and anger which really is self-hatred, self-hatred for his own cowardly behavior.

The religious person may trick his mind that selfless behavior is moral, but he cannot trick the natural biological and rational foundation of his inner self... his true essence as a human being.

"You are magnificent when you accept all of who you are without judgment"

The religious person can never be centered, and in harmony with himself as long as he "acts" selflessly. He lacks self-respect and projects that same lack of respect onto others. He also thinks others can be sacrificed the same way he sacrifices himself.

The anger and resentment he inwardly feels because of his behavior is projected outwardly onto others. He is definitely not compassionate; just the opposite.

What emerges from this picture is the inherent destructiveness of the religious doctrines. The Inquisition, the Dark Ages, the many religious wars are not aberrations but are direct results of following the doctrine of sacrifice, and selflessness.

A contrast exists between the Jewish religion and the Christian religion. The Jewish religion has always held up the individual as the highest value. They do not accept self-sacrifice. That is why the Jews have always been so successful financially.

Christianity introduced self-sacrifice as a major doctrine with Jesus... Jesus who sacrificed his life for the rest of humanity. And even here, the Christian Church misinterpreted Jesus' message.

To use a metaphor concerning selfless behavior, it's like a pot of boiling water on the stove, and the top is tightly closed. The boiling water represents all of your negative emotions you have stifled.

At some point the top is going to explode. Likewise, at some point your suppressed emotions are going to erupt. Examining those emotions makes one realize how destructive sacrifice is to building a moral character.

"You are magnificent when you accept all of who you are without judgment"

When a person becomes serious about religion, it's almost like going through college. You become so intense about learning the subject matter... that's your main focus. You are not questioning the doctrines.

It took me 10 years to break through the selflessness doctrine, at the expense of reaching bankruptcy, and many challenging failures along the way; but all became my greatest assets when I finally broke through.

During the second stage you have rejected a lot of tradition you know is not correct – cutting away a lot of church dogma which has nothing to do with spirituality. After each breakthrough, you reach a higher stage of learning. For example, at the end of the second stage I couldn't say selfishness was right because I was too caught up in religiosity.

Instead, I said there's a higher selfishness... religion instills a strong prejudice against being selfish. A higher selfishness includes the fact that you are moral and honest. You think of selfishness as doing things in your best interest with a sense of being moral. In other words, you don't take advantage of other people. So in my thinking, I turned it into a higher selfishness, which includes fairness and morality.

In actuality there's simply selfishness, not a higher selfishness. People, who think selfishness is cold and does not include compassion, do not grasp the full significance of selfishness. You see, you can't just suddenly make too large a leap in a person's thinking. Selfishness is the opposite of selflessness.

"You are magnificent when you accept all of who you are without judgment"

For religiously oriented people, realizing selfishness is right, is a huge leap. You have to be able to gradually move from one stage of thinking to another. Once you dogmatically stop acting selflessly, and begin to act in your own best interest you build self-confidence. The second stage involves two processes.

One process is becoming goal oriented. You are strongly focused and become very selfish with your time. So two processes are going on at the same time. One in which you practice selfishness, and the other in which you practice selflessness.

The process of being goal oriented builds strength. And through self-knowledge you break with the selflessness hoax. The religious student or mystic enters the third stage with renewed confidence.

He has mastered the major hurdles, the false doctrines which led to psychological turmoil. He has learned to introspect, and trust his own judgment. His new philosophy based on reality gives him a certainty about life. But he has one more hurdle to conquer before he is fully his own master.

He has to break with the idea of God as an external power. During the first two stages you're drawn in so closely by thinking you have communication with God. You really do feel you're having communication with him.

"You are magnificent when you accept all of who you are without judgment"

In the third stage you break with the authority hoax. It took me 10 years before I broke through. During the third stage you have completely broken with dogma but you still believe in an external God. So even though you know self-interest is correct, you still believe you are supposed to do the will of some external God, who is separate from you.

But eventually, it just strikes you. You begin to realize as long as you allow the idea of a God who can tell you what to do, you'll never be your own master, and you'll never reach full accountability for yourself.

You'll never be your own authority. The whole foundation of religion begins to crumble. The communication you thought was coming from God was actually coming from within you... from your own subconscious, your right hemisphere. Finally, I was free to make my own decisions without any obligation to follow the will of an external God.

My first reaction was one of joy, and tremendous relief. There was also certain sadness because the spiritual literature holds out many promises to those who achieve "unity" and none of those would be forthcoming.

Another emotion to work through was the feeling of being disloyal. About one year after this discovery, my new knowledge was put to the test in reality. Would I make my own decisions concerning new directions in my life or would I fall back into the trap of letting blocks to my new direction win out.

"You are magnificent when you accept all of who you are without judgment"

I had made three major decisions concerning vocation, relationship, and what to do with my new knowledge. As obstacles began to appear in all three areas an old emotion surfaced..."to give up desire". A huge emotional crisis took place within me. I experienced tremendous anger at the whole religious field.

During one's study of religious teachings and literature it is constantly stressed how you have to give up personal desires. Over time that leads to a crisis. In the third stage you follow the philosophy of self interest. You build confidence and strength. Yet in trying to follow God's will, you meet obstacles and have to relinquish your will.

So it all eventually comes together in a crisis.

One thing so devastating is that you prided yourself on your intellect. Your intellect does work correctly concerning life, honesty, and being fair to others. All of which is psychology, it's all related to people and you know those things are correct.

Intellectually you have built up a tremendous amount of knowledge and wisdom about life, and people through experiences. But then you still have something else going on, still believing in God and believing you have communication with him. All of a sudden, it's like he's the authority figure telling you "No."

To be your own person, to make your own decisions, you can't have an authority over you. Even the spiritual literature says you eventually give up desire for the spiritual. I'm sure everyone thinks, "Not me, I'll never give up the spiritual." But you do.

For you finally realize you're the one who thought you had communication. But the communication was coming from your own subconscious. This realm is connected to a super quantum consciousness, which we will discuss later in the book.

The reason the student does not recognize the insights as coming from his own brain but thinks they come from outside himself or from God is because the insights are so contradictory to his religious beliefs.

The insights are opposite of his religious thinking... so he does not recognize them as his own. He already believes in God so he projects the insights as coming from God. In the late 1960s, a neurophysiologist, Roger Sperry, carried out experiments on split brain epileptic patients.

Dr. Joseph Bagen did a daring experiment. He cut the corpus callosum between the two hemispheres of the brain which allows the two hemispheres to communicate. He carried out this procedure in severe epileptics, hoping to reduce the severity of the attacks. Then Roger Sperry carried out experiments on the split-brain patients.

When I started reading about Sperry's work, I realized where the communication from God was coming from, the right hemisphere of our brains.

After you break through and realize there is no external God, mystical thoughts, and emotions still linger. For instance, it is stated in the religious literature if you blaspheme against God then something dreadful will happen to you. I felt I should write about my realizations to reveal the truth.

"You are magnificent when you accept all of who you are without judgment"

But then a tremendous feeling of dread came over me. That feeling was the result of religious guilt built into their teachings. I delayed publishing this book, because I made a commitment to myself and to you the reader that I would need to break through this fear, before making this book available.

Intellectually I had to push those feelings away because I knew they belonged to the hoax and had nothing to do with reality. Ironically, the occult preaches self-responsibility whereas religion says to put aside your intellect, and go on faith.

That's what you do when you accept the religious doctrines. You're putting aside your intellect, and giving the religious doctrines a try.

After making the major breakthrough of realizing there is no external God, you also realize those noble desires people have of wanting to be honest, to deal fairly with others, and to be compassionate... all of those desires are coming from within persons themselves.

But as a religious person, you project all of those characteristics onto some mystical God – as if a person is not honorable but God is. You see, it's a real shame people don't claim those ideals for themselves, and hence why the world is filled with low self esteem. Filled with it.

Instead, they project those ideals onto a God, as if by themselves they are incapable of achieving honesty, fairness, compassion.

After realizing there is no external God and wanting to understand the "mystical phenomena" which convinced me I had communication, I began to research studies done on the left and right hemispheres of the brain. According to Evelyn Underhill in her book "Mysticism", the mystical experiences involve voices and visions, also automatic writing.

"You are magnificent when you accept all of who you are without judgment"

In his research, Dr. Wilder Penfield of Montreal, Canada, carried out experiments locating the different areas of the brain and their functions.

Using electrodes, he would stimulate different areas of the right hemisphere of the brain. When he stimulated a certain area within the right hemisphere, subjects would have visions of past experiences.

When stimulating another area of the brain, subjects would hear auditory commands. Dr. Penfield said the auditory commands always sounded like a man's powerful voice. One man said he felt as though it was his father giving him commands.

Even women would hear an authoritative man's voice.

So you see, when primitive people were being guided by the body consciousness mind, they didn't recognize those authoritative voices as coming from their own brain.

It sounds like someone else's voice outside of themselves. So religious and mystical people are fooled. The authoritative voice they hear during those visions is not God, the voice and vision is coming from the right-hemisphere of their brain.

St. Theresa would hear auditory voices. "I heard it once; it was startling. It sounded like a man's voice, very loud. It was late at night, around 10 p.m. The back of my chair faced a corner of the room, so I knew there was no way anyone could be behind my chair. But the auditory voice was so masculine, so authoritative I had to turn around and see if anyone was there".

You don't hear it as you hear me speaking. You hear it inside your head. But it's so strong, as if someone out there has spoken. It's very interesting what takes place in pursuing the religious path.

Roger Sperry wrote in 1966 concerning his split-brain patients that what they experience in their right hemisphere seems to lie entirely outside the realm of experience of their left hemisphere.

The deeply religious student creates on artificial split between his two hemispheres by following the three doctrines of self-sacrifice, giving up personal desire, and following the will of God.

Those three doctrines, those three beliefs, he follows with his left intellectual hemisphere. But his emotional, survival right hemisphere rebels until eventually the right wins through creative insights which reveal how destructive those three doctrines are. It should also be known that singing is a function of the left hemisphere, and singing is very popular in religion because it activates that sphere, it keeps you following and not thinking with your rational right hemisphere.

The core of religion is to perfect character and through perfection help create an ideal society. Yet, as we have seen, the three main doctrines of religion destroy character. Scientific advancements in all fields of science have traditionally conflicted with religious beliefs. Each improvement for mankind has had to contend with religious prejudice.

Religion is a psychological issue. And because psychology is such a young science (starting with Freud in the late 1800s) the average man does not have enough information on what is psychological fact or fiction... what harms him or helps him.

"You are magnificent when you accept all of who you are without judgment"

With the move from body consciousness thinking to conscious thinking 3400 years ago, (which happens to coincide with the fall of "The Holy Temple") man was, for the first time, able to introspect. With introspection a person can decide for himself if something is good for him or bad for him.

But, unfortunately, with consciousness man is also able to deceive himself... to deceive himself with false ideas.

That ability for deception is why religious beliefs still flourish today.

Please understand religion does serve a purpose to some people who really do need structure as a starting point towards the realization of the higher self, we all need to start somewhere... but ultimately it has failed to achieve its true purpose, to be a guide towards the realization of the higher self, the union with the God within.

In the end, all I am saying here is that you need to take responsibility for your own life and make yourself accountable to yourself, and to the world around you to truly reach living a chaos free life.

It's a hard a crude realization to have to make, but when you do, if you have not done so already... you'll understand this statement clearly, and the benefits of living an inner directed life, whereas you activate the God within, instead of the God on the outside of you.

"You are magnificent when you accept all of who you are without judgment"

The key is to be happy

To many, life is random. The reason it is random, it is because if all that energy is left without control (consciousness controls everything), it will be random.

You cannot make a chair without first knowing consciously how to put it together, just the same way you cannot have a child without the integrated process involved. Life driven by chance is the biggest mystical lie of all. There are thousands of pages behind this small book -- too much to write. But the basic principle is this: Let go of the mystical theories and embrace yourself fully.

It starts by developing a sense of self so high, so non-dependent, so unattached to anything, not with an attitude of I am better than everyone, because that is based on relying on external comparison - that is what we need to LET GO OF - THINGS WE GIVE POWER TO EXTERNAL OF OURSELVES, but with an attitude that I want to discover my own unique gifts, potential, and manifest them, not from a sense of altruism or ego, because again that gives power to things outside ourselves, but from a sense of developing God within.

COMPLETE ONENESS.

When one accomplishes this, one will also see the same in others, and extend the same respect, and awe to others.

Why do we experience chaos? We only see outside of ourselves, what is actually within ourselves. When we transform ourselves to be complete within, we can see the perfection that exists outside ourselves.

"You are magnificent when you accept all of who you are without judgment"

Add up many people doing the same and the results of the collective energy will create the only true result of that mathematical equation... Immortal perfection. The formula being: hc/2PIe2

Man has used the theory of an external God for personal gain for thousands of years.

From the days of Nimrod to our modern day nationalism, religion, capitalism.... and those who spoke out were either sent to prison or killed (Jesus, Galileo, DaVinci, and many others), but since 1540 to our modern day, due to advancements in science, and other important factors, ideas that were recorded thousands of years ago, are no longer so farfetched and distant from comprehension.

Even today, some believe chaos has to co-exist with order. Life can't be just good.

I can only speak for me, as for me I rather live my life as Jesus did, free of all the lies, including the lie we tell ourselves that chaos has to coexist with order, that is yet another external thing we give power to, to justify why chaos exist.

Ask a child under 5 years old the question if chaos needs to exist with order and that child won't even know what chaos is.

Why?

Because chaos, even death is a learned mystical lie we keep buying into, when we stop spending consciousness capital for such lies, they will just disappear.

"You are magnificent when you accept all of who you are without judgment"

If you want to choke out the weeds in a field of grass, just plant more grass, you don't have to pull out the weeds, just plant more good grass, the weeds thrive on space, separation, when the grass gets thick enough the weeds automatically choke and disappear.

When the consciousness of immortality becomes more real to more people, chaos won't have any room to exist, neither will death.

When you take on all of life with happiness and joy, you activate your higher inner perfect self, and the more you do it, the more the illusions fall apart, the more they fall apart, the more you activate your Light within.

It's not easy, it is a war…. The only war worth fighting for. Winning this war means the end of all wars, chaos, pain, and the return to our higher Unity, but we will have earned it, we will have created it, and we will have completed the journey we started on with Adam.

The achievement will be that of immortality in a reality filled with love, prosperity and fulfillment.

"You are magnificent when you accept all of who you are without judgment"

It's not the fault of religion

While I spent considerable time talking down to religion, I want to be perfectly clear that any effort spent on blaming anything for any chaos we experience, is the worst kind of external authority we can give life to. We need to take complete responsibility for ourselves, fads come and go and the only reason they exist, is because we want answers outside ourselves.

Today's latest fad is conspiracy theories. Tons of theories about secret societies whose diabolical plan is to enslave humanity. While some of these theories may be true, by focusing on them, by finding yet another external thing to blame, we give life to our own internal secret conspiracy by having yet another distraction that keeps us from awakening the absolute need to take full responsibility for our own selves and how we relate to the affairs of the entire universe. The greatest conspiracy of all is the one that keeps us going in circles constantly finding someone or something to blame for all of life's problems. It is this very vicious cycle of personal distraction that empowers these movements, or influences, to have an iron grip control over the outcome of life.

It is time to wake up and take complete responsibility for our own selves. Everything comes down to being responsible, and accountable within.

Our ideologies, core values, and beliefs could be for all the right reasons and could help us lead a life of doing what is right, but if it causes us to judge other human beings, if it does not bring us closer as humanity... there is no dignity in it. Lack of human dignity, can make the most right things to do, completely wrong. It does not have to be complicated. It's simply a matter of asking ourselves:

"You are magnificent when you accept all of who you are without judgment"

Does this action create unity with another person and dignify him/her as my equal? If the answer is yes... then know you are doing the right things. We don't need a code of law, ideas, religion, political party, etc. to figure out how to inject human dignity in everything. What is human dignity? Putting oneself in someone else's shoes, and appreciating their uniqueness, and making an effort to honor them vs. show them how wrong they are, even if they are in the wrong. Human dignity is powered by unconditional love, and exceptional visionaries of the past and present exude this quality.

Every pain, every chaos we experience is a direct result of how attached we are to the five senses which includes intellect and logic. When we consciously project, or emanate all the feelings, and fulfilling experiences we desire, that is all we will experience, and no matter what happens in the physical world, NO ONE can ever take away from you, what is coming from within you, and projecting outward.

Mind over matter is about living in an undifferentiated state in the mind, where there is no right and wrong... there just is what we conceive into real. Amazingly what happens when we let go of the need to receive from matter, we change how matter acts in our lives and we experience wealth, love, health, happiness, and all the success we could imagine and desire.

The less you care about getting "things" as a way to feel fulfilled, the more you care about emanating those experiences outward for others... the more you tap into a reality frequency of endless possibilities. The sky is not the limit!

Remember you are part of "others" too, so it all starts with you.

"You are magnificent when you accept all of who you are without judgment"

All we experience is how we process the inputs of vibrations and photons, then the same way we've programmed ourselves to accept what "they" said is the correct translation to experiences, we can re-program ourselves to reject the "expected output" and decide it to be whatever we want it to be. If consciousness controls all the physical elements, including time, space and motion, we are only limited to how we interpret everything. If we accept that a wall is solid, we can't walk through it, if we accept that a wall is energy suspended into matter (which means it is not a fixed hard surface) we could walk through walls because we are also the same. It all depends on the programming we've either accepted by "the establishment" or the programming we create that gives us the ability to have mind over matter. It is within our power to do this as individuals, and as a collective.

Taking responsibility for oneself includes the events taking place worldwide, which are theatrical manifestations of our own consciousness. The path to be becoming includes taking complete responsibility for oneself and ALL the outcomes in one's life, but this is not just limited to the immediate results that impact us directly, it includes taking responsibility for how our consciousness manifests worldwide.

Everything taking place in the world today is because a part of us contributes to it; our consciousness gives life to it. War is a result of anger and hatred within ourselves, disease is a result of lack of human dignity in how we treat others or how we perceive others in our consciousness, cancer is a result of separation between each other due to the need to feel more important, or special…. a manifestation of the ego.

When someone passes away at the age of 57 from cancer, I can't help but feel sorrow for in some part, having caused that due to my own elitism, religiosity, or whatever other separatist mentality that is within my split consciousness. We become so busy living, we often forget to give life to a better tomorrow by eradicating the space within caused by the yesterday.

"You are magnificent when you accept all of who you are without judgment"

When we take responsibility for all of reality, and we visualize what life on this planet would be like had we become whole and pure in our own consciousness... we ignite the power to change everything! We end all conspiracies, for the greatest conspiracy is that our ego wants to blame everything that is wrong on the external of ourselves, so every time we spend conscious capital looking for who or what is to blame for our own interpretations, we are distracted from focusing on up-rooting our own negativity within.

How do we get out of this cycle?

Control is a pervasive energy all around us. The moment we are born a birth certificate is issued, the serial number on that birth certificate gets listed as a stock on the world markets, and for thousands of years there have been systems of control in place from nationalism, religion, and so on. All these forces of opposition make up what is known as Satan, and they do serve a purpose in awakening the real you.

Not to mention life experiences from early childhood that replay in our minds over and over. Because of this pervasive energy we tend to distrust and try to control how much we are giving or taking, but in reality all we truly desire is to be in control of how we act in situations.

We either choose to give more of ourselves, or give less, when we choose to give less but the situation requires we give more, we experience being taken advantage of... however, this is just the left hemisphere of our mind giving feedback. Recognizing this, helps to use our consciousness to activate the right hemisphere of our mind. It is also important to realize that everything we experience we have created for a good reason, that is to say that the very situation that seems out of your hands, may be something you want to experience so you can pro-actively activate the right hemisphere and choose to not feel taken advantage of, but rather become a being of sharing, caring, and giving more of yourself... for in doing so, you will experience the very thing you are willing to give.

"You are magnificent when you accept all of who you are without judgment"

The world around us is a theater that plays out our consciousness. In our heart of heart we want to be beings of influence of positive energy, but just like any game to become really good at it, we need to compete with the opposing team, only in losing to the competitions can we learn our weaknesses and work to overcome them, which means we can never lose because every situations helps us grow and become better and stronger. That opposing force is what creates the illusion of the need to control, and the blame game, but it's only playing that role so you can overcome it.... because what you really want is to be in control of your reactions and become a being of emanations by earning it through this competitive game within yourself. So the challenges that come your way are nothing more than a theatrical play of a game in place with opposing forces, to help you overcome them. That force is known as Satan, but just like the concept of God, it is not an external being outside of you, it is within you.

Say for example someone desires their soulmate, but for some strange reason they keep getting into relationships that are simply painful; who said that a soulmate would be peaches and cream? If we desire our soulmate for the sake of receiving from it, we are going to be let down over and over and over, however if we desire our soulmate for the sake of being able to give more of ourself, to help that soulmate grow and be there for them, then when that person is asking more and more from you, you are excited about it, because you truly are with your soulmate, the one who is helping you become a being of sharing. By having this consciousness by the way, we attract like minded people who will do the same in return, and if already married... you'll be amazed on how the person you are with becomes someone else... You'll think he's changed; when in reality all that has changed is your own consciousness and response to situations.

"You are magnificent when you accept all of who you are without judgment"

Any pain we experience is simply a reflection of how much we are willing to give of ourselves or not. When we are willing to give, we see everything as an opportunity to elevate ourselves to be becoming, however when we seek to receive, especially from other people, we are going to live a very painfully disappointing life. The answer is within your consciousness and what you truly desire; to be a creator/giver, or a container/taker. It is your free will choice to make every day.

Quantum science has proven that if one, just one of the vibrational and photon echoes within the whole spectrum changes, the entire resonance of the entire collective changes. So, as long as we are busy fixing the collective, we are distracted as to the only way to fix the collective, which is to fix ourselves which contains within the entire collective. Of course, critical mass makes a difference, but as long as we are focused on the critical mass, we stop focusing on fixing ourselves, and cannot accomplish the task. Every time we change a negative trait within, it helps change someone else, and each piece of the puzzle comes together to form the whole picture.

It is so important to go deeper into the pain within, because otherwise we keep trimming the weeds, but we don't get deep enough to the roots. Our body consciousness does not like to do this, but our higher self awakes every time we go against the nature to avoid challenges, or blame everything external to our own self. This pain that we experience... this pain that needs to be healed in all of us... it is nothing but the illusion that we are separate... when we heal ourselves... we heal the whole... we are ONE!

"You are magnificent when you accept all of who you are without judgment"

In conclusion, it's never the other person's fault, the conspiracy's fault, the fault of religion, the fault of God, or the fault of Satan... it is always a question of our own commitment to take full responsibility for ourselves, which is taking personal responsibility for everything external to us, it's never the other way around. Everything exists within ourselves, both the energy known as God, and the energy known as Satan.

The other way around exists only because we give life to it, it's a way to excuse ourselves from being accountable.

As long as we are spending time blaming, we are distracted from identifying the negative traits we need to uproot within that will help us become magnificent, and we'll then see that the world is a magnificent place too.

Remember, the forces of opposition exist to activate the God within, those forces of opposition are called Satan; Satan is not someone with horns who wants to destroy you, it is a force of opposition... we put in motion that force when we decided to earn our Light to become creators, instead of created. That force is not your enemy, it is the force that helps you overcome defaulting to laziness, and irresponsibility it is the force that brings you to religion so that you could eventually realize the hoax and break free, it is the force that causes all your challenges so you can overcome them and activate the God-Man within you.

That force is your ally in becoming the real you. To some of you, reading this may sound scary, even wrong... but that is the trick of that force, it has created a double bind, a catch 22 for you, but not to keep you in the pits of hell, but to help you wake up and walk out of hell on your own, to help you tap into your higher self, to help you awaken the real you.

"You are magnificent when you accept all of who you are without judgment"

What we can learn about Quantum Consciousness from 9/11

I was leaving the Viacom building in Times Square to go to my PricewaterhouseCoopers office on 6th Avenue, when I saw all the faces looking downtown along Broadway. I looked up on the jumbo screen, I looked down Broadway and saw it with my own eyes; as I watched I saw the second plane hit the second tower, and the Pentagon crash on the jumbo screens and the overall experience was terror. I have never cried as hard as I did on that day.

Five peers perished that day... they were on the planes, I did not fly for almost 3 months after that; considering I was on a plane 2-4 times a week. I saw 12 years of work with clients in those buildings, not to mention thousands of lives, go up in smoke and remember saying there must be something I can do. At the time I played a role with the City of New York in the clean up process, by setting up a team of auditors to make sure contractors were not defrauding the tax payers.

Today I know, that I was partly responsible for what happened due to my lack of human dignity, and I know I am partly responsible for much of the chaos in the world... for the same reason. Quantum Consciousness is very powerful... you never know when you act a certain way towards someone, the butterfly effect it has across the world. I try to inject love, compassion, and understanding in all my dealings... but my reactive actions manifest will all the pain in the world. It's my fault, and yours too. I am thankful that every day I live, I have an opportunity to change myself which changes the world to be a better place for all of us. I desire for all to join me in this endeavor.

You may wonder why I take responsibility for what happened and why you should too.

"You are magnificent when you accept all of who you are without judgment"

Quantum Consciousness is very powerful. We hear and read about consciousness, awakening, love, compassion, unity, understanding and so on, regularly today; but it's not enough to just talk about it, be aware of it and desire it. Consciousness conceives, governs, constructs and becomes existence. Transforms the is not, into what is. Who directs consciousness? You and Me.

All existence is ultimately controlled and evolved through volitional human consciousness for its self-expression.

Human consciousness is the eternal integrator and controller of existence. Human consciousness ultimately controls the relationships and geometries of the other existence modes -- matter and energy along with space and time. The human-consciousness mode is the purposeful, unmoved mover of existence.

In plain English: What you and I desire is what becomes expressed into existence. If you and I are not happy with the world around us, we MUST review our desires because we created that world... WE CAN ALSO CHANGE IT TO BECOME WHAT IS NOT TODAY INTO WHAT IS TOMORROW.

That's great so, all I have to do is desire and everything will come into existence magically?

No. Desire without action creates nothing. So this begs the question, if I desire a cure for aging, but I am not a scientist or doctor how in the world am I going to take action to see this desire realized?

"You are magnificent when you accept all of who you are without judgment"

That's the amazing thing about Quantum Consciousness, it is a collective of energy we put out and it gets manifested through the domain owners who have influence, and can take action on the collective desires; however for the right information to download to that domain owner, we each have to give 100% to the domain we each own. Meaning, if I am a janitor I need to care about what I do and give 100% of myself to the job I am fulfilling, for this action, which is within my domain of influence, will activate the power of my desires that are within the domain of influence of someone else. The same applies in the opposite direction. If I am a scientist working on a nano technology delivery system that can reverse the process of aging, which is my domain of influence, only when I give 100% to this endevour will I activate my desire for a better dust sweeper device to clean my lab, which is in the domain of influence of the janitor.

Whatever we desire, only becomes existence through the domain owners that have the unique gifts to create the output of our desires, but only in giving 100% to our own domain which we have the unique gifts to create the output for others desires, can this become possible.

Conversely, when we act with lack of human dignity, when we find ourselves saying things like: "I can't stand that guy, he is such an idiot, I wish he would suffer", or whatever other negative thought/desire we have towards another human being... that desire/thought MUST also manifest. How?

The world/existence is a theater for the playing out of our desires/consciousness. Read that again please!

For example: The Middle East is a theater playing out our lack of human dignity locally, wherever locally may be for you. The genocides of history were theaters playing out our thoughts/desires, and actions. 9/11 was a theatrical manifestation of lack of human dignity in China, or Russia, or South Africa, or Chicago, or Los Angeles, or elsewhere.

Just because something does not play out locally, just because the theater of our Consciousness does not impact us immediately or directly locally... it does not mean that it won't play out, and manifest into reality somewhere else in the world, because the political leaders of the world are also influenced by the Quantum Consciousness of all of us; they are owners of a domain of influence that can have global complications or benefits, and the input of their output/actions comes from our Quantum Consciousness. It's easy to complain about a leader who is doing all the wrong things, but it's not so easy to admit that you and I are causing the theater to play out based on our own individual Consciousness that becomes our collective Quantum Consciousness.

Our individual Consciousness, and actions adds weight to the Global Quantum Consciousness and it will always become manifested through the domain owners of influence that will put on the movie, the manifestation, the theater of that Consciousness somewhere in this world.

So, let's get down to the basics.

How do I take responsibility for what is happening in the world all around me if I am not the domain owner of influence of the manifestation of those actions? In other words, I am not a scientists so how can I influence finding the cure to cancer, aging, even death?

Simple.

Check in with your desires on a regular basis, if they are small, desire for bigger desires, and whatever domain you have influential ownership of... give 100% to it by focusing on injecting human dignity, love, compassion, understanding, and unity in all your thoughts, and actions.

For example: If you are an artist, give 100% to your domain of influence by focusing on your craft as a means to provide me pleasure, because that will give power to your Consciousness that will add weight to the Global Quantum Consciousness, so that those who can influence your desires (world peace), will get the insight to do so. If you are a CEO, give 100% to your job by making sure your company adds value globally and that your products, and services always take into account human dignity first, value for people, for the world, for the Universe, because that will give power to your Consciousnesses that will add weight to the Global Quantum Consciousness, so that those who can influence your desires (a cure to diabetes), will get the insight to do so.

"You are magnificent when you accept all of who you are without judgment"

Conversely, unfortunately there are plenty of dark forces and dark energy we've put out there and agents of these forces ready to manifest chaos, but we can choke those out the moment we decide to let someone drive in front of us, vs. giving them the finger or assuming we have the right to be in that lane; the moment we finish something we started, even if it means giving so much of ourselves to it that it sets us back temporarily (which is an illusion), and the moment we take complete responsibility for ourselves and for each other.

Get the picture?

We individually are responsible for becoming complete within by giving 100% to our domain of influence, for one simple reason... to make it possible for everyone else to do the same, for another simple reason... because the outcome of our existence depends on it. We need each other, but only in taking complete responsibility for our own domain of influence can we truly show in action that we care about each other, knowing that we are activating the power of Quantum Consciousness and having certainty that just as we are giving 100% to our own domain of influence, so are others in this world.

Any lack of confidence in humanity, in political leaders, in anything and everything, is a direct reflection of our lack of giving 100% to our own domain of influence, with human dignity, compassion, love, understanding and unity. Only by completing our own fragmented puzzle piece can we offer up a piece that will fit with all the others, only in completing our own piece can we empower the rest to do the same.

"You are magnificent when you accept all of who you are without judgment"

Human dignity is proven in not only how we deal with each other, but how productive we are with ourselves and by giving 100% to our own unique gifts and talents. I dignify you, by dignifying my own role in the world, and vice versa.

In the end, it does not matter who did what to whom, what matters is that it happened. Period.

Why did it happen?

Because it really is up to you and up to me, individually, to become aware of the power, and the grand responsibility we have to effect positive change in the greatest theater of manifested Quantum Consciousness.... EXISTENCE.

"You are magnificent when you accept all of who you are without judgment"

Why fears set in right before we are about to break through

We spoke about fear in a previous chapter, but why does fear set in? Is it real? Is it a warning? How do we overcome it?

Often we reach a cross road in life where we begin to have fears, most of the time evolving around thought patterns such as: Can I do this? What if I fail? I don't think I have what it takes? What will others think? and so on...

These fears have nothing to do with the actual reasoning going on in the mind, it is the opposite. We don't fear failure, we fear success.

We often fear becoming a success, or becoming "the go to" person.

Why?

Because when you become that person, there is no turning back, and you have to be willing to take criticism, which is where you learn a great deal about yourself, and compliments which tests your ego into thinking you've accomplished something, and that is when you stop growing; constantly balancing knowing you are amazing, with humility acknowledging that everyone is amazing.

A client, who can easily be the next Ralph Lauren, learned just how unproductive he has been for over 25 years. Our first 72 hour "Awareness" process (Described in The Four Phases to Success, in my book "Unlocking Your Empire") helped him discover that he is only productive 3 hours and 20 mins a day.

"You are magnificent when you accept all of who you are without judgment"

So I said: I have good news and bad news; the good news is I can show you how to get everything you've done in the past 25 years in 3 hours and 20 minutes, and you can spend the rest of your day lounging around, the bad news is you won't become what you want to become being productive only 3 hours and 20 minutes a day, worse you won't feel fulfilled.

So we started to put in place the mini-week work day (it is a methodology that allows you to get a week's worth of work in one day, also in my book "Unlocking Your Empire) and he began to see that this new process was going to help hold himself very accountable to himself first, and everything around him as well; he finally saw a system that could help him achieve his goals.

Something peculiar happened going into week 3, he froze. One of the things I discuss with my clients is to be totally honest, and open with oneself. After a little discussion, he admitted he was afraid to become who he wants to become, because he realized his life would change forever, and in the end, he admitted "I am afraid to succeed" or as he put it: "I am F..ing Scared"

The story of his new chapter continues, but I wanted to share with you, the importance of realizing that most of the times we fear being successful, becoming who we are meant to be, not failing.

Also failing is not such a bad thing, especially when you realize what it really is "another successful wrong approach". If science was scared of failing, we would have made no advancements at all, science finds solutions in the process of elimination, failure is built into the success equation of science, and it should be no different in your life.

DO EVERYTHING WITH CERTAINTY AND WITHOUT FEAR! No matter what happens, you will be one step closer to living life as the real you. Nelson Mandela said: "It is not our darkness that we fear, but the Light within us".

"You are magnificent when you accept all of who you are without judgment"

Transforming the world impossible to I aM Possible

During the first phase of conscious humanity, what economists call the Agricultural age, life was predominantly based on survival by growing crops and feeding from the fruit of the land. Any conflict was a direct result of who had the better more prosperous plot of land, and who wanted more without earning it. Then came the industrial age, where progress was based on machines doing a great deal of the work, and initially those machines were used to continue to support the agricultural age and these were dark times, jobless times… until the fight to hold on to the old ways of doing things ended, and people who were struggling through those hard times awakened to the possibility of a new world, and embraced it; some became extraordinarily wealthy, I don't have to say their names, it does not take rocket sciences to figure out who they are. Just look at your appliances, the car you drive, and so on… The names are in front of you everywhere. Then came the information age around 1970.

Before the industrial age, and the information age some conscious beings spoke of a world where you could transport yourself across the world instantly, live forever, prosper, be healthy, never get old, and where life would be nirvana.

These men were stoned, flayed alive, crucified, hung, and killed for speaking a language that did not make sense at the time.

Especially since they spoke of the activating forces of making all that possible, love, compassion, forgiveness and understanding. They spoke of the concept you are reading in this book "activating God within".

"You are magnificent when you accept all of who you are without judgment"

At that time, during the Roman empire, those qualities were severely lacking… the world was very political, very much about getting rich at the expense of others; life was not valued as precious, and the highest honor was to be a soldier, an assassin for Caesar. Here came a few conscious men, GIANTS among men, who spoke of love, compassion, forgiveness, understanding, unity… imagine speaking to a civilization that did not value those things, about the importance of them. Can you blame that civilization for reacting as they did? Can you excuse them?

Now imagine someone came to you 200 years before the shift of the agricultural age and said to you: "You know soon you'll be able to have automatic machines that will water your crops, and you'll be able to harvest a thousand times faster using machines, and you'll be able to make better use of your land by having machines that will turn the soil faster, so you can get more crops out of every season". The response was: You are evil, these things are an abomination, and you are a witch and a sorcerer.

It's kind of ridiculous to read this kind of response today, but that was the response back then.

Fast forward a little bit and you find yourself during the Newton era, Galileo, Copernicus, and many other brilliant minds, who spoke of the laws of relativity, quantum science, that the earth was not the center of the Universe, but rather the Sun was the center of the galaxy, and the earth was round, vs. flat and it was held into space, not by some mystical elephant creature.

These people too were thrown in jail, ex-communicated by their religious groups, etc. Yet to conceive any other reality about the Universe today, sounds absurd, and ridiculous… but only 300-500 years ago what we know to be the truth today was scorned at and rejected.

Fast forward some more and you find yourself close to 100 years ago, predictions were made of being able to speak across great distances instantly, being able to travel to space, vaccines that could extend life, cure most disease that were the killer diseases of the time. I mean polio... who thinks about polio today? Not too long ago people died from polio, it was as lethal as cancer is today, yet a vaccine was found and that disease was eradicated from existence; those people were thought to be insane too, and were ex-communicated by their religions, persecuted, even killed.

Each transition in the evolution of Consciousness of humanity was met with tremendous resistance, and rightfully so. Imagine you had invested your life into what you held to be your truth and the economy was based on it, and here comes some revolutionary thinker threatening your very existence and survival with ideas that are totally opposite of what you have been lead to believe as truth.

Think about it, you just read the idea that there is an energy of opposition called the Satan that is designed to help you awaken the real you. Religion teaches that this force is a being that wants to destroy you. Religion also thought that the world was flat, and stoned to death anyone who stated otherwise. I mean they put Galileo in jail for most of his life. Galileo is a hero in our modern day, yet back then he was the working of Satan, as religion teaches Satan to be.

Just know that progress does not wait for people to decide to progress, it happens ready or not. The order of the Universe and the Energy of the Light moves us forward as part of the bigger plan, resistance is futile. If someone can conceive an idea, there is truth in it... ideas exist only because they can be materialized. We'll cover this a bit later in the book.

"You are magnificent when you accept all of who you are without judgment"

Each shift in ages, or phases of the evolution of Conscious humanity was met with great challenges, like the great depression for example before the explosion of the industrial age… the industrial age had started in the 1500s, yet it really did not take off until a major depression took place in the 1930, 400 years after the beginning of the industrial revolution. We had 400 years to get it right, but the only way we finally got it was through a major depression.

Today, no one questions our ability to talk to anyone across the world instantly, we have mobile phones, we have Twitter, Facebook, we have Skype, and we have video cams. I mean the prediction of teleportation, has already come true. Space exploration is already in progress, vaccines to major deadly diseases of the past are already the norm of today. Not too long ago, the very things that we as humanity used to say "Only God can do that", and rejected ideas from giants of science, and giants of philosophy, which can be summed up as giants of spirituality today; we are doing them.

God is within us when we transform the word impossible to I aM Possible. The master plan was to become Creators, God-Man, that is why we put this messy reality we are in, in motion to begin with. The Bible speaks that we were created in His image, and with His attributes.

What if the metaphors were to enable us to consciously awaken to the possibilities of being able to do anything we can imagine as good for the advancements of humanity, and shape it into reality? I mean today we have childhood super heroes like Superman, Spiderman, The Fantastic Four and so on… when we were kids we used to imagine being able to fly, and leap across buildings.

"You are magnificent when you accept all of who you are without judgment"

These God like superheroes gave us the ability to dream and think beyond our limited body consciousness. The stories of the superheroes of the Bible are no different, and the ultimate superhero able to do anything and everything, is God. But Jesus said "God is within you"… Are we living in a limited mind set, because we don't think we have what it takes to create a better tomorrow?

I mean who invented the word "Impossible" to begin with? Maybe it was meant to be I aM Possible in disguise. The point isn't to discuss the Bible or God for that matter, we've done enough of that in previous chapters, the point is to awaken that if any one of us is waiting for a miracle to happen, we are no different than those who resisted and rejected the changes that were occurring from the agricultural age, to the industrial age, to the information age.

So what is next?

We are undergoing crises all over the place, be it financial, our eco system… let's face it, we have used up a great deal of natural resources with no regard for the effect or outcome on the future, just to stay in an age (industrial) that must come to an end. World conflicts over oil, religious views, borders, even conflicts over monetary systems, are just ridiculous. It's time to move on from this phase, founded on a control the masses agenda, and to embrace the next phase, the next shift of human ascension.

"You are magnificent when you accept all of who you are without judgment"

The age of unification with God – the ultimate expression of Super Universal Consciousness

I like to call it the Age of the Entrepreneur; after all, entrepreneurs have been around since the beginning of time. You may have heard of King Solomon, King David and many prosperous conscious entrepreneurs of the past, whose kingdom reflected a state of abundance and prosperity for all. Why? They used Light Consciousness in their thinking, and more importantly in their actions.

Agriculture kept us alive, machines allowed us to envision becoming more productive, computers allowed us to automate machines and make them intelligent, information allowed us to become aware of things we were in the dark about, cloud computing has introduces the ability to quantum analyze data instantly, getting to answers sooner than later… enabling the discoveries of the near future, and social media is converging humanity as one.

The near future, which wont' take 300-500 years like the last shift we experienced, will happen within our generation. That future will be the dawning of technology advancements like nano technology, where stem cells will provide the answers, and technology will enable a delivery system of nanobots into our blood stream that can proactively repair cells atomic and subatomic structure. We have already split the atom, why not find a way for the atoms (which are immortal) to keep sustaining life in a healthy body?

"You are magnificent when you accept all of who you are without judgment"

Science has already discovered that if our bone segments, which are very hollow today, were filled with liquid diamonds, we could withstand G forces (meaning fall off a building and walk away unscathed like you were Neo in the Matrix). Nano technology and soon to be discovered delivery systems will make all of this possible. We wills soon wake up to a world without disease, without aging, without death. A society exploring across galaxies to bring the awe and love we uncovered for each other to those worlds… bringing stem cell based nano technology into non living planets today, and turning them into habitable paradises. This is the future I want for my children, a future full of possibilities not impossibility, a future where the norm is to think I aM POSSIBLE.

If you think it's a pipe dream, just review history… the men who predicted this kind of world were called dreamers, rebels, evil, etc. Two men who lived in that reality 2000 years ago were Jesus and R. Shimon bar Yochai. It's a shame how much of what they predicted, has been taken out of context by the very institutions that have tried to keep humanity from leaping forward through each phase. The Torah is full of stories of Conscious beings, who did not live life on automatic pilot, going from filling one desire to the next, to the next (give me, give me, give me), but beings who suffered and endured.. which is nothing more than a code for beings who were introspective, and who practiced proactive restriction which allowed them to be connected to their Higher Self, the Unity with God.

When you turn on a light bulb, what allows it to be bright is the filament; the more tightly wound the filament {restriction} is, the brighter the bulb.

When we seek to be filled by external stimulations, we are living life without a filament, as if we are on automatic pilot, worse asleep. There is nothing wrong with anything that is called "bad" today; seriously there is nothing morally wrong with drugs, alcohol, sex, etc , except that they don't work long term to make us feel fulfilled, and the other problem is that when we are busy filling ourselves to be happy (be it drugs, no string attached sex, drinking too much, partying, getting rich at all costs, buying stuff to make us feel better, seeking relaxation, fun) we are missing out on awakening ourselves to the future, worse on awakening ourselves from playing an integral part of that future… a future where I aM POSSIBLE.

Even just sitting around feeling content, is the same thing as being busy doing the things society calls "bad". Yes being a good person, is just as if we are doing the "bad" things. Anything that keeps us feeling good and comfortable that comes from the outside in, is a distraction from awakening the higher self. The God-Man, who is directed from the inside out.

When we restrict our desires to be filled, to be comfortable, it awakens the desire to emanate. To eat deliciously steamed vegetables, you first have to let the pressure cooker build enough steam and pressure to apply the benefits of it into steaming the vegetables. When we restrict our ego based desired to be filled, we allow our internal energy, the Light within us of possibilities, to give birth to anything we can emanate outward. By not restricting our ego, we have nothing to share, and happiness comes from sharing, so if we have not allowed the Light to build up, the filament is too weak to generate a bright Light in our lives and the world, and since happiness comes from sharing it, emanating it… how can we emanate what we have not allowed to build up inside us, through restriction of the ego?

This is why it is so important to not just focus on becoming great, but to restrict our desire to be served by the sabotage robots; you will read about in a later chapter, to allow ourselves to be becoming magnificent beings of possibilities, who truly honor "God", by allowing that force to become active within us.

We all need to re-think the old ways and operating systems, and embrace becoming Light Conscious driven beings. Light Conscious driven being make decisions with the effect in mind. The new society of Light Conscious entrepreneurs think about what is good for the self, the employee, the shareholder, the customer and humanity... but go a step further, they think and act in ways that fosters advancement in the Universe, they are not limited by any boundaries, other than to have enough time to break them for the sake of benefitting the whole collective. If you are undergoing financial hardship, challenges, anything that stops you on your tracks and forces you to introspect (or get depressed – your choice really), if you don't see it as a gift, an opportunity, a merit to be able to step into the reality of the future, you are missing the all point of it.

Every major advancement has come out of a major depression. Why? Because when enough people introspect, and restrict the give me give me give me mode of operation, something miraculous happens to them... they come in contact with their higher self, their magnificent soul who is a spark of the Super Universal Consciousness we call Light... God Consciousness! I went through it, when I had no ability to buy things that used to make me happy, or even run away from challenges, it was as if I was in a pressure cooker, locked in a prison... but I came to realize, I was actually becoming free, awakened to transforming the impossible, to I M Possible, I was allowing the Light within to build up.

"You are magnificent when you accept all of who you are without judgment"

The current present is going to be the past of the future, and the future will tell the story on how we handled the present. Do you have an idea that can benefit humanity? Are you pursuing it, regardless of the challenges? If the answer to question 1 is no, you are too busy filling yourself with happiness, vs. seeking to emanate it and are operating in a faulty mode that will soon be a thing of the past. If you said yes to the 1st question, but no to the 2nd, why would you miss out on being the cause of the future society, or worse defaulting back to the old operating system.

When we are not pushing ourselves beyond our comfort zone, we are defaulting to the obsolete past. We have only the choice to go forward or backwards… there is no standing still.

Becoming a Light Conscious focused being requires a leap forward in not only thinking, but in action…

It's time to re-think, re-calibrate, and change everything, vs. adopting the past into the future… each leap has been so huge, why expect it to be any different this time?

You know its coming; you can experience it inside you. You can feel it.

We are too busy trying to solve problems using old operating systems that simply no longer work. For example, if you have a great service or product, and someone else has a great service or product and you both could benefit from it, why allow lack of funding, or money to be the deciding factor on you moving forward or not… one thing of the past operating systems that still works is "bartering". A resource based economy fosters growth without limitations of currency of a capitalist economy. People helping people. Wow what a concept… some things just never go out of style, and some ideals are true no matter what age we are in.

This is why the only operating system that will work in the future, is the original one intended for humanity, a system based on love, compassion, understanding, unity, and convergence.

This operating system is known to some as Nirvana, to others as The Messiah. You and I are the activators of this operating system, the ones who get to boot it up.

How?

It's all about restricting the things that sabotage the system, the viruses of the old operating system based on give me, give me, and give me. That system is pre-dos, I want the post Windows, and Linux system, I want the grid nano technology processing system… don't you?

"You are magnificent when you accept all of who you are without judgment"

Overcoming the need to be served by external energies

We are at the most elementary level energy and energy flows. Energy is not static, so it either flows into well defined containers we create that drive a positive outcome, or it flows into containers that hold us back from succeeding, which is also an outcome. Or it can just flow...

Since energy is not static, energy is always flowing, it is either flowing to serve in a positive way, or it is flowing to serve you in a negative way. Energy in its self has no purpose without something that can manifest it. It is how many containers or vessels we end up deploying in our lives that control the outcome of our lives. Many of these can include things like: depression, procrastination, sadness, anger, resentment, and judgment, let's call it the container of energy known as: "sabotage robots".

Yes, our body consciousness likes to be served, so when nothing that we perceive as good is serving us we turn to those robots we've created called "sabotage". Our body consciousness reasons like this: I can't afford that new toy right now, because I don't have the money working for me and therefore I don't have the means to fill my need for happiness right now, so I am going to have sadness serve me because I need something to fill me, something to give me energy... and it does, there is energy in sadness, depression, anger, resentment, judgment... they are sources of incredible energy; those energy containers are not external of you, you created them and put them on reserves to come and serve you when you are feeling low on energy... so you deploy those robots who come and give you the feeling of control.

"You are magnificent when you accept all of who you are without judgment"

Activating the real you, requires first coming face to face with all your addictions, the energy you've put into containers (call them robots) who come to serve you on demand. This realization causes one of three things: Flight, Freeze, or Fight responses. Those who choose to fight, one by one begin to realize that leading a measurably productive, and accountable life is about pouring energy outward not only into containers, but into pipes that drive the progress and improvement of humanity, because the more you seek to be served, the more the other robots (sabotage robots) are given life to live. When you become inner to outer directed, with the purpose of being a value creator for others, those sabotage robots begin to die.

When you are planting a lawn, the best way to kill the weeds, isn't to pull them... weeds thrive on space; plant more healthy seeds and as the good grass thickens the weeds choke and die automatically, because you are removing space. The way you live a chaos free life, is by removing the space between the good grass (the energy pipes we pour our essence into for the sake of being a value creator) and the bad grass (the energy containers we pour our essence into for the sake of serving us when we are not willing to be value creators).

It's very simple actually, what you give energy to determines your state of mind, and the related actions you take determine your mood, if you are not producing, you are taking. The robots in the taking mode of operation are: One time shots/blast of energy such as, alcohol, drugs, no strings attached sex, anger, resentment, depression, doubts... that are intended to fill an emptiness within, that emptiness cannot be filled from the outside, it can only be filled by planting more good grass... or by emanating energy.

"You are magnificent when you accept all of who you are without judgment"

Yes even relying on positive inputs such as a new car, a new house, a new experience, allows for the negative inputs to exist. Seeking to receive energy from anything coming from the outside in, is a form of sabotage, it does not only have to be anger, resentment, depression, doubts, etc... It can also be the need to party on the weekend, the need to have the latest gadget, the need to be fashionable, for without them we feel empty. Notice, I said "need", there is a difference between "having" things, and "needing" them to feel happy. You should desire to have everything.

Now you may ask, how do you fill a void without filling it? That is the point, you don't fill voids, you remove the space between the good energy you put out and the voids, by giving more positive energy outward. Only by emanating what we desire to experience, can we actually experience it. The void does not need to be filled; it needs to simply be eliminated by creating more outwardly focused pipes of energy. If you have a plot of land that is empty, you don't fill it with grown fruit trees, for they might live one season and die the next, you plant the seed, water it, and then you let something called nature take its course. The seed of the trees are then rooted and participate in the process of growth in the plot of land they were planted in, they were not transplants, and hence they can keep giving fruit, year after year.

When you create those pipes, all you do is plant the seed, and water (work towards the realization of those goals) but the actual outcome is not within your hands, the outcome already exists, just like a fruit tree is already existent within the seed, but how it manifest and produces fruit is based on the farmer's actions, and then the course of nature, which sustains the tree.

"You are magnificent when you accept all of who you are without judgment"

All around us there is energy which we are a sub-set of, recognizing this principle will allow us to one by one, remove the space in our lives, and stop asking the "sabotage" robots to come to our aid when we feel empty, but rather we begin to plant more positive seeds, (take more actions) realizing that we can be absolutely certain that whatever we plant, the outcome already exists in the Universal Consciousness. We just have the merit to benefit from the process. The reward isn't the outcome; the reward is being able to play a role in the process. Being a value creator isn't based on waiting for the end result to be happy, because that is again a "sabotage" robot we are creating, it is in just being in the process. To be becoming!

It is in becoming, that the real fulfillment comes from, and this is the difference between creators/leaders, and takers/followers. A real creator is happy being a creator, and if out of 1000 efforts one is a huge success, the outcome is a bonus to a creator not the source of the fulfillment.

Whenever you begin to get frustrated with how long a process is taking, saddened by that lost deal, resentful of having given more than you got back, judgmental of how people work and behave... remember this: You are asking the sabotage robots to come to your rescue and in doing so you are allowing space to continue to exist... you are contributing to your own chaos and that my friends is unfortunately contributing to the chaos of the world. To remove the weeds from the world, we must first remove our own void/space that we fill with chaos robots we give power to.

"You are magnificent when you accept all of who you are without judgment"

Redefine success not by the outcome, but by how challenging the process is... the more challenging, the more you are doing exactly what you need to be doing to be a value creator in society. The more challenging it is, the greater the revelation of how much void/space you have to overcome within yourself, and as you remove that space the sabotage robots begin to choke and die. Yes, the challenge is nothing more than a revelation of how much void/space you have in your life, between your positive actions (energy you put out) and your negative actions (energy you seek to pour in), most people spend time getting rid of the external things that they think causes the void, but the void exists because we poured energy into it. We gave value to sadness as a source of energy; we gave value to doubt as a source of energy, we gave value to anger as a source of energy... All these negative energies exist, not due to some external evil force that created them, they exist because we keep giving energy to them, and we desire to be served, vs. desiring to serve.

The next time you are feeling the sabotage robots knocking at your door, realize you created them to fill the space within you, and by allowing them in, you keep recreating that space, you keep giving power to the very thing you desire so much to remove. Shifting from being takers to givers, reveals the true purpose of challenges; opportunities to help you unify with your higher self by removing the weeds from within yourself, which we have already learned cannot be removed by pulling them out, they can only be removed by choking them out.

The more you become a force of emanation, the less you rely on attraction to be happy. As long as we are attracting, filling our own vessel, there will be a risk of the energy coming in, and since it is not static, it will empty out too, this causes the ups and down of life.

"You are magnificent when you accept all of who you are without judgment"

However, if we shift from needing to attract, to emanating... becoming that force of all we desire is the gift. Receiving everything is about emanating all we desire because the ultimate energy, The Light, it is not static; it flows through people who become pipes of energy, not containers. Our job is to become good farmers, by planting, watering (taking the actions in a systematic way) and allowing nature (The Light) to pour life into everything we do that produces the fruits that will benefit others, and thus sustaining the cycle of creation and recreation which is endlessly fulfilling.

You must learn about your weeds, and recognize how you keep them alive, how you keep the void/space alive. Do you use sabotage robots in the form of anger, resentment, jealousy, fear, doubts, depression, worthlessness, and so on? You can't remove the space, until you see it for what it is, and one by one remove its source of energy from its very existence... the sabotage robots we empower to keep that void/space in existence.

The only way we can achieve total fulfillment is by emanating all we desire, love, happiness, success, health, life... as long as we are a container ourselves, we can only achieve so much, because it is limited by a container, but as long as we become a pipe, the energy that flows through and outward to benefit not only ourselves, but others is endless.

The ultimate removal of space is death itself. Death exists, because we give it power, when we as a whole focus on becoming givers, emanators of Light energy, the vaccine for death itself will be revealed, for life is the normal mode of existence, not death... void/space = death.

"You are magnificent when you accept all of who you are without judgment"

So next time your own sabotage robots come knocking at your door, know this: If the angel of death came knocking at your door, would you let him in? Of course not, so why allow his agents (space/void/chaos) in? They come in by way of needing to be served, vs. becoming beings of service.

Remembering this simple principle, when they come knocking, can give you the strength you need to repel the need to be served, and become a being of service. However, just emanating positive energy is not enough, you must see and acknowledge the void/space within and seek to find how you keep it alive, and one by one, work on those sabotage robots, while you also work on emanating positive energy.... We must work on both at the same time... and this is not a task for mere mortals, hence the desire for immortality must stem from the desire to remove all the space of humanity, it starts within and it extends outward. Otherwise the desire for immortality is nothing more than another external thing we want to serve our own ego.

The ultimate desire is not to achieve fulfillment, because that is actually the normal state of existence, but to merit working on removing the space between our current state of (give me, give me, give me) receiving, to the state of fulfillment which is (give, give give) to become a being of emanations, emanation of Light.

To participate in helping humanity step into that reality where there is no time, space, or motion. It starts with you, it starts with me, it effects you, it effects me... it's removing our internal space, to remove the space between us.

It's about us; it's about UNITY bonded by the anti-space: LOVE. Love is a verb, it's an action. Everything we experience is an action we put into motion.

"You are magnificent when you accept all of who you are without judgment"

Everything is controlled by you

We create the moods we are in, and can alter them with a few simple steps and understanding.

Running a successful business, being a contributing employee, being a good leader... requires mastery of emotions/moods. Happiness, appreciation, excitement draws money in (and everything else for that matter), anger, sadness, lack of appreciation pushes money away. Why? Money is energy and like attracts like, money is good energy and it flows where good energy is welcomed, and where the energy will also get re-distributed (shared), but it's not about money, entrepreneurs create wealth by being willing to give up short term flow of money, to create greater opening for the long term.

Ultimately you need to create a container or a vessel for the money to flow into, and this at time requires going without it for a little while to allow self transformation and sometimes the complete reinvention of the self. Building a container is not enough, because your ability to fill it, is limited to the size of the container, building a pipe is better... a pipe feeds others and is always full. Energy, what makes up everything in existence, flows and is always expanding, it does not stay static. If you fill a container with energy, it will eventually need to flow out of the container and this puts you at risk of having moments of emptiness, but if you build a pipe that fills other containers... energy will always flow through you endlessly. When everyone in the world starts to build pipes, energy will flow endlessly to all, there will never be any emptiness, ever. More on this topic in a later chapter.

"You are magnificent when you accept all of who you are without judgment"

Many entrepreneurs went bankrupt, some even spent time in jail (BF Goodridge) because of their bankruptcies, many of them lived with very limited means… but they were making money all along the way by creating a container, actually a pipe for wealth… and they gave so much of themselves that eventually they became the giants of our times and created empires for generations to benefit from. So if you are giving all you have to an idea that will benefit society, but you are not making money at it (for now) in the form of currency, don't assume you are not creating wealth for your future, your family, your grandchildren, and opportunities for countless other families and generations.

It is important to see beyond the here and now of today, to create the exceptional future here and now of tomorrow.

Society defines success as fame, fortune and achievement as perceived through the eyes of others. We convince ourselves that we will be happy when we finally make our fortune, find the perfect spouse, graduate college, or end up at the top of our business. But most people who define success in these terms are unhappy, and will likely remain this way, unless they change.

Happiness comes from within, and emanates outward. It's a verb, an action, something you do, not get. There are some principles that can serve as a map that will lead us to true inner happiness. In life's journey, our natural feelings of peace, love and joy frequently become clouded by the negative forces inside us and beliefs or illusions we've allowed along the way due to external exposures.

"You are magnificent when you accept all of who you are without judgment"

These negative forces we've allowed to create the illusion of our own reality easily enslave us, and our subsequent reactions to them usually cause a negative outcome (or a loss of joy). Built up stress and insecurity can be eliminated by understanding how we become slaves to our thoughts systems. Notice I said systems, not system. Why? Because there are two types of inputs that become thoughts in our minds, one system is connected to the Universal Consciousness of endless possibilities; the other system is connected to the illusionary "I Can't" realm. Both systems feed the mind all day long, one is more powerful than the other, and this is the only thing you can control…. Which one you allow to be more powerful to you.

You don't control the thoughts, because you don't generate them, we discussed in an earlier chapter the concept of domain owners and Quantum Consciousness… but you do control which system you activate in your mind, based on your behaviors, which at times need to go against the input system of the thoughts that come from the "I Can't Realm"…

It is really important to understand this concept, for most of us believe we control our thoughts, and that is part of the illusion the "I can't" realm of thoughts feeds us, so we are blind to what is really going on.

We can control the signal and the amplification of the signal of the right thought system that comes from the Universal Consciousness of endless possibilities, also known as "The Endless World", "The Light", "God",

"The Higher Self"

To keep it simple, there are two thoughts input systems that your mind tunes into; one comes from the real you, the other from your fears.

Truly, thoughts determine attitudes. However, most people believe they are victims of their thoughts or worse creators of them. We create the output of all that is around us based on our ability to filter through the constant input that comes from either our soul, or our ego. In science this is often referred to as the right vs. left brain hemisphere, or the bi-cameral mind. However, while there are two radio stations constantly transmitting positive and negative thoughts, it is up to us to choose which signal to act upon. You can act upon the signal from Light FM, or Dark AM, both are transmitting all day long, and both do serve a purpose in awakening the real you, as we have already discussed.

Controlling your thoughts is about knowing how to tune into the right signal. This simple shift in thinking can be very revealing of our own happiness because there are no victims in life, just those listening and acting based on the input from the right radio station and those not. At times the signal is fuzzy, when you are not sure which input you are listening to, it's actually Dark AM, and it often broadcasts in the form of noise and fuzziness.

We can think anything we choose to accept as a thought for us, and our emotions are then a direct result of what we choose to accept as a thought that we take action on.

Our mind is constantly justifying why we create a feeling, and then because of our five senses we convince ourselves that they are real and we become slaves to the feelings we created based on the input we accepted from the thought radio stations. It is truly sad when we begin to believe the lies broadcasting from Dark AM as our reality. But that is the point of the game, to overcome that opposing signal.

"You are magnificent when you accept all of who you are without judgment"

If you think life is overwhelming at times, it cannot be. Only what you accept to think about life is overwhelming, not life itself. The simple solution? If you don't like the feelings what you are thinking about, stop thinking about them, and stop tuning into that station. Your ego loves that station, but the real you does not, so take control of your thoughts instead of allowing them to control you, because your thoughts will lead into actions, and actions control moods.

How is this done when the feelings are so strong? Try viewing feelings as an indicator or a compass. Negative feelings tell us it is time to dismiss negative thoughts. Positive feelings tell us we are experiencing life through our soul consciousness. How do you know when you are tuned into the Light, and when you are not related to your feelings? If the feeling comes first, it is from the soul, if the feeling comes after some "calculation", it is from your thought system called the ego, and even that can be distorted if you are not actively tuning into the right station.

Each of us interprets life differently. The reasons become obvious when we understand that everyone sees through the filters of his or her own unique consciousness (thought system). But when we stop judging (input from Dark AM /Ego) and start appreciating people's differences (input from Light FM / Soul), we can learn a great deal about ourselves from them.

Why? Because we are all linked, we all came from the same place, and each of us although different, is uniquely interdependent on each other. When the world understands this principle, there will be peace and life will never cease to exist. Wait, so immortality is possible? As long as there is no more threat of hatred, discovering the vaccine for death itself is not only possible, but it already exists. It is broadcasting on the Light FM radio station, but to hear it… we must shut down Dark AM completely, and this is a collective effort of humanity. Shut down Dark AM! How? By not acting on the thoughts broadcast of Dark AM.

"You are magnificent when you accept all of who you are without judgment"

Any form of condemnatory judgment, hatred, or self-righteousness only contaminates the consciousness of our soul that could lead to positive action. It's as if we have the Light on in a room, but we cover our eyes so we can't see it. Conversely, higher levels of understanding will come natural from positive feelings that surface when judgmental thoughts about separate realities are dismissed. We raise our consciousness every time we dismiss judgment of others.

When we are in a high mood we see things one way, when we are in a low mood we see the same things differently. For example, you are at the checkout line of your favorite food grocer, and your Light consciousness would let someone go in front of you, perhaps because he/she is in a hurry and only has 2 items. However, if your ego consciousness takes over, you may reason with yourself, I am in a hurry too, we are all in a hurry, he/she can wait like the rest of us.

Now imagine, you walk out the store and strangely enough you get into some kind of accident that you might have avoided because you were in the store an extra 5 minutes.

Sometimes we are given opportunities to alter the outcome of our life in a positive way (Light FM is saying... let this person check out before you do), but we let our ego (Dark AM is saying… your time is just as important don't let this person check out before you do) thought system take over and ruin it for is. We don't often see the logic and perfection to an otherwise chaotic life, because we are only tapped into logic, but the real logic is happening when we can see beyond logic. Chaos is an illusion, everything is perfectly balanced we just need to learn to tap into it. We tap into it with our actions, not thoughts.

"You are magnificent when you accept all of who you are without judgment"

Gratitude can help in altering a bad mood too. Just by appreciating your health, talents, children or simply a beautiful object, you begin to want to give rather than receive. Expecting something back for any good deed you do is manipulative, conditional giving, it is driven by the ego. Really be thankful, and share without expectations, it will do wonders to improve your mood, and amplify Light FM in your life.

Becoming beings of sharing and caring is the only way to drown out the noise from Dark AM, and the more we do it, the more tuned in we become to Light FM, the more we improve our mood.

Your mood is the biggest determining factor of your success in anything. Your mood is the outcome of which thought you decide to act on, and the thought you are tuned into is the outcome of the inwardly outwardly directed life you choose (that of Love, Truth, Honesty or Hate, Lies, Dishonesty).

Most think that our thoughts and mood direct our actions, it is very much so the opposite... Which thoughts we allow ourselves to act on is what impacts our mood.

"You are magnificent when you accept all of who you are without judgment"

Life is like a puzzle, all the pieces are perfect but only fit a certain way

Remember as a kid when you purchased a puzzle and started putting it together? Some had 100s of pieces, some as many as a thousand. The more majestic the picture, the more complex the puzzle. What came first, the puzzle or the picture?

The picture of course. The fun was putting the fragmented picture together so as to recreate the picture, you knew all the pieces fit together in a specific way, but you had to discover which way, in the process of recreating the picture. I don't know about you, but there were times I believed the pieces were wrong, the company that created the puzzle had to have made a mistake for sure; this at times lead me to give up on the puzzle till I was ready to try again, and sometimes I never tried again, I just believed it was wrong and gave up trying.

Unfortunately at times we experience this in life, we have the end picture of what could be, we've seen it, felt it inside ourselves, but in the process of assembling all the pieces of the puzzle together "to get there", we begin to have doubts that we don't have the right pieces, and give up.

The bigger the goals, the more majestic the outcome, the more complex the puzzle is; requiring patience, perseverance and absolute certainty that it will come together. This begs the question. Is the result a combination of efforts, or does the result already exist, and it requires integrated combination of efforts to reveal/manifest it?

"You are magnificent when you accept all of who you are without judgment"

When you go into a room, which is wired with electricity, is the electricity already there, or does it happen when you flip the switch on? The electricity is there, the wiring is in place, the bulb works… you just take the action of flipping the switch and the room lights up.

The result in anything you wish to manifest is already in place, but it's up to you to take the necessary steps, and actions to see it through.

The results of your ideas are already in place; otherwise you would not have had the thought, insight, intuition, vision to do what you do to begin with. This is an important concept to understand: "The outcome exists before the thought, and the integrated actions to manifest it already exist, you just need to persevere in putting them all together". The solution to a problem exists, before the problem comes up, so does the process to solve it.

So where is the solution, the outcome, the manifestation? It's in a potential state, fragmented like the pieces of a puzzle. The picture already exists, but it's fragmented into 100s, or 1000s of puzzle pieces you need to put together. In life, to manifest the end goal; you have to defragment all the pieces that go into.

How do you put together the fragmented pieces of your life? By integrating time with actions, otherwise it just sits in a potential state. This integration of actions is called "PRODUCTIVITY".

The laws of productivity, and applied consciousness in every thought, action, time and speed, is the biggest contributing factor behind the success of the most well known people in the world.

"You are magnificent when you accept all of who you are without judgment"

Energy has patterns, and different tasks consist of different energy-patterns. When one mixes two or more different integrations of energy-patterns together by shifting from one task to another, or from one responsibility to another without any controlled structure, interferences of energy occur, and energy becomes wasted without ever being converted into something of value.

This happens in your personal life, your business life, in the world around you, and across the entire universe (just imagine what would happen if the order of the universe was off by even a nano-fraction of a second).

Take something as simple as a chair; it was consciously designed out of the desire for something to sit on, but the composition of a chair required the conscious integration and use of nature's resources (wood or metal), individual need (I want something to sit on), global benefits (everyone needs something to sit on), and business outcome (everyone will buy a chair).

What gave birth to the chair is the conscious integration of all 4 values: Personal, Business, Global, and Universal.

Ok, so let's say you have the knowledge, you have the system, but you are stuck. Getting back to the puzzle, what stops someone from believing they can assemble the puzzle, or worse what makes a person think they can't, or start to have disbelief that the pieces are just wrong; the puzzle can't be assembled because the puzzle maker screwed up?

Life experiences can often shape how we perceive ourselves as a piece of the puzzle ourselves, and how we fit in the bigger puzzle called humanity. We don't see how all the pieces DO FIT TOGETHER, often because we are fragmented within ourselves. There is fragmentation outside of us, because of the fragmentation within ourselves. So how does one break free of this illusion? You have to be willing to see and re-trace where the fragmentation started, and you can't do it alone. Work with a friend, a mentor, a teacher, a therapist… someone you trust to help you see aspects of yourself that are blocked.

Stop for a moment focusing all your energy in being great, and try to see the garbage you are holding on to that blocks you from being magnificent.

I spent 7 weeks with one of my mentors, teacher and friend retracing where I gave away sparks of my own essence, worse how when I gave those sparks away, I created a movie where I acted as the victim, the piece of the puzzle that just doesn't fit (I really brought into that illusion for many years). I listed 40 life events that had a profound negative impact on my life, dating back to as early as the age of 2. I made a list of all those events, wrote how they made me feel, and then one by one, I discussed them and relived them (ouch!). In re-experiencing all those painful events, I began to see sparks of my essence I gave away, so I took them back and also saw the masks, and new illusion based realities I created to close/protect myself from being hurt (I created a jail cell for myself).

"You are magnificent when you accept all of who you are without judgment"

Some of those masks manifested by being obnoxious, manipulative, and downright dishonest, all because I felt like all the pieces were wrong, except for me, why? To protect myself from hurting, while continuing a vicious cycle of sabotage. Interestingly enough a theme emerged by the end of the 7 weeks, which allowed me to forgive myself of all the guilt, shame, and to forgive all those involved too… actually I came to love and thank them for what their real purpose was, "to open within me the willingness to give more than I receive in life".

Some of you might be asking how do you thank someone who robbed you? How do you thank someone who cheated on you? How do you thank someone who abused you? How do you thank someone who molested you? How do you thank someone who bankrupted you? How do you thank someone who spread lies, and rumors about you? And why is this important in life?

First of all, no one can do any of those things to you, how you experience everything is based on your own attainment of consciousness (or lack thereof) and perception of reality. To achieve anything in life, you must be willing to give all you have to it, but not for the sake of achieving the goal, or being a good person, or helping others; for the sake of activating that force within, the end result is a byproduct, a bonus, but the real joy comes from embracing the process.

The fun of a puzzle is the challenge in putting together all the pieces!

"You are magnificent when you accept all of who you are without judgment"

Happiness, love, success, these are all verbs, meaning they are forces that go outward from within, not inward from the outside. As you retrace your experiences, you begin to see that the reason someone outside yourself is mean to you, is because they are in so much pain, they strike first to protect themselves from being hurt, or they want so much from you because they are so empty and lost; you learn to look beyond the appearances, and appreciate that you are in that situation to give more of yourself, and that the other person is simply crying out for love. It does not excuse their behavior, but how you experience it is within your control. There is much more to this, this is just one aspect of it.

Imagine a world full of people willing to give more of themselves – we would have no poverty, no wars, no fragmentation…. We are heading in that direction, we don't have a choice anymore, and we must get there, for our very life depends on this.

The blissful end result already exists in everything we do, if we are not there yet, it is because we are locked up in a potential state. Why? We need to give more to it than we are willing to, even when the rewards for giving more to it are not immediate. The truth is, the reward is in the giving more, for that activates a force inside us that is truly the secret to living richly in every way... We need to keep trying to put the pieces together, even if we doubt they will fit, we need certainty that the end picture is inherit in all the puzzle pieces.

Activating the real you, requires to let that magnificent being come to life and direct your life.

"You are magnificent when you accept all of who you are without judgment"

Activating success in all we do, is not about having the best idea, or "knowing" the best theory, wisdom, technology that will remove the fragmentation in building your business, your relationships, and humanity as a whole… it's about taking "action", integrated fluid productive actions with persistence, patience while having certainty that all the pieces DO FIT TOGETHER, even the ones that just seem so wrong. Being open to this, having an open heart allows the individual to see the puzzle pieces clearly, unfragmented and that is one of the secrets to succeeding at anything.

In business you reward a good employee with more responsibility because he/she has the ability to take an idea, and execute actions that produce the required results. You give them puzzles and they put them together, no matter how difficult the puzzle is. As an entrepreneur or organizational leader, it is important to remember that although you might be the boss, you are also the employee. The idea, the vision, the result is already in place, not because you came up with it, but because you have the skills necessary to put it all together to benefit others, conscious of it or not.

As a God-Man you are both your Creator and the created.

This does not mean it will come easy, because in the process of realizing that goal there is something you need to learn about yourself, improve about yourself. A good leader is one who is always keeping in mind that he has to be the first to change, evolve and improve him/herself, for this is how he/she will help others become better too. Inspiration comes by way of example and by caring about the people that have voluntarily brought into your vision, and dedicate a substantial amount of their time and life, seeing it through.

"You are magnificent when you accept all of who you are without judgment"

What are you doing to help them succeed? If you want people to take your lead, then you must learn to be lead.

Every major CEO or leader always has an advisor behind the scene. Why? Because entrusting in another person your fears, concerns and limitations is asking them to show you, what you can't see within yourself. By being open to seeing the garbage, you can burn it and reveal your greatness.

Working with a mentor, an advisor, a trusted friend on a personal level, is critical to growing and putting all the pieces of the puzzle together correctly, it's not a sign of lack of abilities, it is a sign of maturity and knowing that as much as you know, there is also so much more you don't know about yourself. Asking someone to show you the things about yourself you can't see is the best investment you can make in yourself and in the world around you.

Everything comes down to relationships, improve the relationship you have with your higher self, and that will extend outward into everything you do, ask someone you trust to tell you honestly the traits you need to improve, be open to change, humble to learn, embrace the process… something amazing will happen, you will begin to see everything flourish around you, and the puzzle come together in the right order, at the right time, revealing the greatness of the real you.

"You are magnificent when you accept all of who you are without judgment"

Embrace all of who you are

Everything we do starts from the left hemisphere of our mind, when it's a positive action we harmonize the right hemisphere (the place our Light lives, the power to reason based on knowledge and honesty) and thus this creates health within our body (the central hemisphere where everything is manifested), and that body extends to the bigger body called humanity, and the Universe.

The trick is to admit to oneself, where ALL motivation comes from and still love oneself for having the biggest ego in the world... because the bigger the ego, the bigger the potential for revealing your essence and your Light.

The more in touch you are with your ego, the closer you get to your Light.

It's a shame most religions and spiritual systems focus so much attention on removing the ego, or making you feel bad for being alive in a reality of judgment and flaws, that is like saying remove your desire to live... whereas the focus should be in transforming the ego into the desire to become a source of motivation to share your essence, and reveal your Light, and to add to the energy of Expansion (what many refer to God) towards emanating and bestowing love, compassion, understanding, joy and all that is fulfilling onto others, which starts with the self.

"You are magnificent when you accept all of who you are without judgment"

Everything we have is a spark of Light, including that nasty habit we beat ourselves up for having, and allow it to keep us from achieving greatness for the sake of adding values onto others. It's ok to accept oneself as is, but to not accept the as is, as an excuse from becoming what we are meant to be.

Behind every motivation, there is a mixture of purity and total ego, and there is no such thing as total ego, because while the conscious intention might be self absorbed, the subconscious intentions (aware of it or not) is to reveal Light, even if that Light is in the form of darkness for someone, due to your actions, which in the end helps them get to revealing their own Light and essence.

Nothing is a mistake... so why live like part of you is great and part of you is a mess, just embrace all of you and keep going, keep trying harder and keep believing that your purpose is to become a being with the power of bestowing good onto the world, that is ultimately the real you in a state of potential that only you can manifest.

How?

By accepting your good and your bad, as power sources for revealing your greatness for the sake of changing the world to a greater place for all of us. By using the mind of a winner and by applying the principles in becoming your own hero we discussed earlier in this book.

"You are magnificent when you accept all of who you are without judgment"

Lack is an illusion. We never lack anything

We never lack anything at all. Whatever the situation is that we are in, even when we have chaos in our lives, there is something we are getting from the situation, we may not be aware of it (consciously) but we are getting something from the circumstances we are in, otherwise we would not be in them.

When wondering why we are "stuck" in certain situations, remember... we are never stuck. We are getting energy from being in that situation. We get energy from the reasons we aren't making millions, aren't with our soulmates, aren't healthy, or whatever other "aren't" we individually are dealing with. Remember reading about the sabotage robots?

Why does this happen?

Because we value the situation we are in, more than the energy we would get from changing the situation. At the end of the day we are energy, and we are always full, it's a matter of understanding what motivates us, but we are never at the mercy of anything but our desires, or lack thereof and the actions we take to realize them or not.

Everything starts with desire, but desire without actions is just that... desire. What we manifest in our lives is a reflection of our strongest desires, conscious and unconscious, followed by our actions, voluntary or robotic.

Knowing this can help us shift into parallel universes instantly, when we decide to swap out what we are manifesting at this moment, with what we truly desire to manifest and take actions in that direction.

"You are magnificent when you accept all of who you are without judgment"

Acceptance - The secret to shifting into a parallel universe of love

You can only extend to others what you value within yourself. If you embrace yourself even when you are out of sorts or worse in sabotage mode... you'll extend the same courtesy to others when they are in the same mode.

Conversely, when you accept yourself as a gift in the world, the real you will recognize the same in others and you'll see the same in others. Whatever is external of you is who you are within. If you don't like what is external of you, simply shift what is within you, change yourself.

"ALL PROBLEMS SOLVED". Simple right? Not exactly.

When you just can't seem to be able to make that shift... don't avoid or mask your darkness, go deeper in the darkness you are in to discover the source of it, but stop beating or judging yourself up for being in it, ... the Universe chose you to play out the darkness so you could overcome it and create the frequency for others to do the same.

YOU HAVE BEEN CHOSEN TO OVERCOME THE DARKNESS YOU ARE IN.

But how?

The way out of hell in life... is on the other side of it. The door is just past the point of no return... only those trusting that the door is within reach, can walk through fire and gain control over everything.

"You are magnificent when you accept all of who you are without judgment"

What does that mean exactly?

There are two ways to overcome challenges in life.

1) You work really hard to transform yourself, and to overcome the "not so good" traits; most of us end up simply suppressing who we are, but few do actually transform "some" aspects of themselves. You can pull the weeds.

2) You accept yourself as you are, and you focus on becoming a being who bestows goodness in the world. When you are feeling bad about yourself, you are not good to you or anyone. Kind of a bummer way to live right? You can plant more good grass.

The first route will have you chasing your tail for years, and when you do fall (which happens in this imperfect reality) you'll feel so bad, that you can't focus on anything else. This has been the cause of depression, anger, resentment and all the chaos in the world for thousands of years. It all stems from lack of self respect, self love, self dignity, self honor, and lack of self acceptance.

It's impossible to accept others as they are when we still have elements we don't accept about our selves. Think about that for a moment. Why do certain traits about others bother you? Because they remind you of traits about you that you don't accept. How can you accept other people's traits, if you don't accept yourself completely?

"You are magnificent when you accept all of who you are without judgment"

The second route shifts you into a parallel universe instantly, where you begin to accept others by allowing them to not be perfect, just like you. When you accept yourself for all of who you are, you can do the same for others, and you also begin to experience life's beauty and perfection in the imperfection.

What a concept!

Something amazing happens within the second route. As you remove judgment from yourself, you remove it from the world... as judgment diminishes, so does chaos. Chaos is energized by judgment, remove judgment within, and experience a world without chaos or cause and effect. Yes, accepting the worse case scenarios in the world will actually shift the entire world into this parallel universe and due to the removal of judgment those worse case scenarios will simply cease to exist. If judgment powers up chaos, remove the judgment and chaos will cease to have any source of energy.

Acceptance shifts you into a parallel Universe where bliss is the normal mode of existence... Acceptance is being present without judgment.

You'll likely experience certain people leaving you, and the right people surrounding you instantly when you make this kind of shift in your life, so don't get too upset when certain people no longer seek you out, there is a reason they are not part of your life anymore, they are not living in the same reality as you are, but accept the fact that someday they will, don't judge!

This chaos free reality is waiting for you, want to join me?

"You are magnificent when you accept all of who you are without judgment"

Give yourself a hug and say: "I am great just as I am, and I love me just as I am; I extend the same to everyone around me, and allow them to accept me as I am. I can now focus my energy on emanating the love I have for myself to the entire world, and allow the world to do the same in return".

Most of the chaos that exists is due to judgment and hatred for no reason, but it all starts within. Why does judgment exist? Because of lack of self love.

If we loved ourselves enough, just as we are... we would extend the same to the outside world and in turn activate the energy of mercy and love which knows no chaos.

For millenniums we've been chasing our tails, going in circle feeling bad about our "character flaws", which in some ways has kept us from achieving our greatest potential as humanity.

It's important to get in touch with our own inner ugliness, yes... this is very important, but for no other reason than to recognize it, accept it, and find love for ourselves even with it.... this in turn allows us to extend the same courtesy to others, and more importantly the less life we give to it, the more it will dissipate within, and all over the world.

We often think free will is about our ability to choose right from wrong, but this is completely off. Why? Because the natural order of things is perfection, bliss, order, harmony... that is the normal state of existence.

So why do we not experience it all the time?

"You are magnificent when you accept all of who you are without judgment"

How we choose to perceive ourselves, is how we experience the entire Universe... the only free will we have, is to choose to accept everything with love or with judgment. That's it.

When we judge ourselves and others, we choose to use our free will to diminish the reality of bliss, into a sub reality of chaos. When we love ourselves and others (as we are, and as they are), we choose to let the flow of Light be pervasive and we tap into harmony, and bliss. Notice I said tap into, not create... because the reality of harmony and bliss has always existed, we have chosen to diminish it due to our judgmental nature.

Every action we take is part of a master plan beyond our immediate control, however when we choose to accept and love everything as is, we step into a reality some call Nirvana, The Messiah, or the Endless. It' all starts with how we use our free will.

Judge or Love vs. Right or Wrong.

Right or wrong exists within the realm of judgment, therefore while we think we are exercising free will, we are not... we are robotic within the realm of judgment.

Love exists within the realm of the Light. Our true free will is only exercised when we choose Love over Judgment, which translates to the end of chaos.

Our thoughts and actions generate energy; this energy multiplies and creates a frequency for others to tap into. The more we generate the energy of compassion, love, and we shed a tear for those who suffer, the more a sense of urgency will take place worldwide to do the same.

"You are magnificent when you accept all of who you are without judgment"

Imagine enough people doing that? We would usher in the end of all chaos.

It is pure Quantum Consciousness.

Every dimension is a reflection of the other; however when you change just one, it also reflects onto the others. We exist within a 10 dimensional model, which has 10 dimensions within each dimension and this is multiplied infinitely.

You and I are one element of these dimensions, but we have something unique: "Consciousness" which controls every dimension, so when we shift our consciousness and reflect it in our actions in any directions, the rest of the Universe complies with our thoughts and actions.

In fact there is a constant on energy that supports us, the energy of expansion (aka GOD), and this energy takes our consciousness and expands it. This energy does not judge which direction our consciousness goes, it just supports what we want. Remember the idea of the satellite?

Religion has made this energy a judge of good and bad, hence why so many problems in the world, because we look at things from a place of right or wrong, vs. from a place of what is expanding, and asking ourselves if that is what we really want?

This energy we call God/Light/Universe is ready 24/7 to support what we want to manifest through our consciousness. We are that powerful as human beings. So, the more we put out the proper frequency, the less chaos.

Hence the question every one of us should ask is: What can God do for me?

"You are magnificent when you accept all of who you are without judgment"

Many grow up thinking this energy called God wants us to do something for it, it's quite the opposite. You cannot give the energy of expansion anything, it is constantly expanding and lacking nothing.... this is our whole purpose, to get to the same state... beings of constant giving and lacking nothing. It all starts with a thought that materializes into an action, which creates a frequency that materializes into reality. What reality do you want to create?

Here is the secret to gaining control over your life, you've been waiting to read about. To explain it, I am going to ask you to think about a situation in your life you need to analyze. I want you to think of it as a picture in your mind, build all the characters involved in your mind, and construct the reality of the situation in your mind.

Now I want you to put all those characters in motion and play out various scenarios in your mind on the best approach to deal with the situation, play out all the scenarios, erase and redraw the scenarios that did not pan out well. Change the actions of each character in the thought constructed reality of your mind, and see them act differently each time, until you see the thought through to its perfect state and result.

How long did that thought take in your mind? A few seconds, perhaps a minute at best?

Now imagine if those characters were like avatars, real characters, how long was that thought constructed reality for them? If you recall you had the characters change, act differently, interact with the entire thought process differently each time, until you reached the perfected outcome in your mind. If those characters were real, to them your instant thought felt like years, perhaps lifetimes.

Hold on to that thinking for a second before you read the last pages.

"You are magnificent when you accept all of who you are without judgment"

We are all in the middle of a thought. Our collective consciousness has constructed a reality that needs to be perfected, we are the characters drawn in and out of this reality, acting differently within each drawn up construct, being erased and redrawn, over and over until we work through all the issues to bring the thought into a perfected blissful result.

None of what we experience is real, our bodies are characters within the constructed reality of our collective consciousness, and lifetime after lifetime, for millenniums we've been working diligently to perfect within this construct (physical reality) what we have already perfected in our consciousness.

Our purpose as humanity, which has felt like thousands of years, when in reality within our collective consciousness is a thought taking less than a few seconds, is to perfect this physical reality to match up to our collective consciousness reality, which is already perfect and chaos free.

The purpose is to become in this physical realm that which we already are in our collective consciousness – God.

The real you is not the summation of the character in this illusionary construct, it is the architect and creator that is drawing you in and out of existence in this construct, trying to shape your physical self into perfection, along with everyone one else.

We created a system of opposition on purpose, to make it challenging to assemble the puzzle, but the end picture already exists, yet part of the opposition we created was to forget this fact, but as we get closer and closer to finishing the job, we are beginning to remember.

"You are magnificent when you accept all of who you are without judgment"

This critical realization allows you to overcome any challenges in this reality, because you know that the real you is already living chaos free, all you have to do is let that real you guide you in this physical realm. All you have to do is unify your materialized self with your non-materialized immortal self, with your own architect and creator.

When the collective of humanity reaches this understanding, we will begin to act accordingly towards one another; we will begin to seek to collaborate with each other in completing the thought: To match our perfect state of existence in our consciousness within this physical dimension.

You can proactively connect to your perfect self at will and redraw your reality at will, and snap another piece of the puzzle into place... we can all do that and reach our fullest potential where we will be able to say to each other:

Welcome to Nirvana, the Messiah Consciousness, the Endless Reality.

Welcome to the Real You.

ISBN #: 978-0-557-47300-7

Author: Tullio Siragusa

Publisher: Lulu.com

Rights Owner: Tullio Siragusa

Copyright: © 2010 Tullio Siragusa

Language: English

Country: United States

Edition: 1st Edition © 2010 Tullio Siragusa

Suggested Soft Cover Retail: $19.99

Connect with the author on Twitter: @tulliosiragusa

ISBN 978-0-557-47300-7
9 780557 473007
90000

"You are magnificent when you accept all of who you are without judgment"

Lightning Source UK Ltd.
Milton Keynes UK
UKHW010648250320
360870UK00001B/124